Intellectual Property Law in South Korea

Intellectual Property Law in South Korea

CHO Youngsun

This book was originally published as a monograph in the International Encyclopaedia of Laws/Intellectual Property Law.

General Editors: Roger Blanpain, Frank Hendrickx
Volume Editor: Hendrik Vanhees

Wolters Kluwer
Law & Business

Published by:
Kluwer Law International
PO Box 316
2400 AH Alphen aan den Rijn
The Netherlands
Website: www.kluwerlaw.com

Sold and distributed in North, Central and South America by:
Aspen Publishers, Inc.
7201 McKinney Circle
Frederick, MD 21704
United States of America
Email: customer.service@aspenpublishers.com

Sold and distributed in all other countries by:
Turpin Distribution Services Ltd.
Stratton Business Park
Pegasus Drive, Biggleswade
Bedfordshire SG18 8TQ
United Kingdom
Email: kluwerlaw@turpin-distribution.com

ISBN 978-90-411-60096

This title is available on www.kluwerlawonline.com

The Author

Professor Cho, Youngsun (born 19 September 1966) teaches intellectual property law at Korea University School of Law in South Korea. He obtained degree in law from Korea University (1988). After thirteen years' work as a judge in Patent Court and other District Courts, he began his career as a professor at his *alma mater* from 2008 onwards. He also taught IP law in an Executive LLM programme of University of Washington in St. Louis (summer, 2010). As an IP law commentator, he authored a patent law textbook running into 4th edition and co-authored several commentary books. He was a national member for WIPO's Asian-Pacific IP judges' colloquium (2006), and served as vice president of Korean Patent Law Academy (2011). He also acts as Chief of a Patent Act Renovation Committee in Korean Intellectual Property Office as of 2014.

The Author

Table of Contents

The Author 3

List of Abbreviations 21

General Introduction 23

§1. General Background 23
I. Geography 23
II. Cultural Background 24
III. Political System 24
A. Constitution 24
B. Division of Power 24
1. Legislative Branch 24
2. Executive Branch (President and Cabinet) 25
3. Judiciary 25

§2. Judicial System 25
I. Legal System and Jurisdictions of Courts 25
II. Appointment of Judges 26
III. Proceedings 26
A. Civil Proceedings 26
B. Criminal Proceedings 27
IV. Judicial Process of Intellectual Property Right Dispute 27
A. Tribunal in KIPO (Korean Intellectual Property Office) 27
B. Appeal to Patent Court 28
C. Infringement Suit 28

Chapter 1. Copyright and Neighbouring Rights 30

§1. Sources: Legislation 30

§2. Subject Matter of Protection 31
I. Works 31
II. Works Excluded From Protection 32
A. Governmental Works 32
B. Current News Reports Transmitting Simple Facts 32

C. Program Language, Protocol, and Solutions 32
III. Special Categories of Works 33
A. Special Subjects Listed in Copyright Act 33
1. Derivative Work 33
2. Compilation Work 33
3. Cinematographic Work 34
B. Special Subjects of Theoretical Matters 35
1. Applied Arts 35
2. Computer Program 35
3. Database 35
4. Character 36
5. Works against Order of Public 36

§3. Conditions of Protection 36
I. Formal Requirements 36
II. Creativity 36
A. Substance of Creativity Requirement 36
B. Creativity in Functional Works 37
C. De Facto Standard and Creativity 37
D. Scènes à Faire and Creativity 37

§4. Ownership 37
I. General Rule 37
II. Joint Authorship 38
A. Conditions of Joint Authorship 38
B. Effect of Joint Authorship 38
III. Employee's Work 38
A. Definition 38
B. Ownership of Copyright for Employee's Work 38

§5. Transfer 39
I. Assignment 39
II. License 39

§6. Scope of Exclusive Rights 40
I. Moral Rights 40
A. Substances of Moral Rights 40
1. Right of Disclosure 40
2. Right of Attribution 40
3. Right of Integrity 41
B. Relevant Norms 41
1. Inalienability 41
2. Prohibition of Defaming Use of a Work 41
3. Revision, Addition, or Reduction of Work 41
II. Property Rights 42
A. Right of Reproduction 42
1. Definition 42

2. Decision of Plagiarism 42
B. Right of Public Performance 43
C. Right of Public Transmission 43
1. Broadcasting Right 43
2. Internet Transmission Right 44
3. Digital Audio Transmission Right 44
D. Exhibition Right 44
E. Distribution Right 45
1. In General 45
2. Exhaustion 45
3. Exhaustion and Parallel Import 45
F. Rental Right 46
G. Right of Making Derivative Works 46

§7. LIMITATIONS OR EXEMPTIONS TO THE SCOPE OF COPYRIGHT PROTECTION 46
I. Limitations of Moral Rights 47
A. Limitations of Attribution Rights 47
B. Limitation of Integrity Right 47
II. Limitations of Property Rights 47
A. Reproduction for Judicial Proceedings, Etc. 47
B. Use of Political Speech, Etc. 47
C. Use for Purpose of School Education 48
D. Use for Current News Reporting 48
E. Reproduction, Etc., of Current News Articles or Editorials 49
F. Quotation from Works Made Public 49
1. Conditions of Fair Quotation 49
2. Internet Search Service and Court's Lenient Interpretation of *Quotation* 49
G. Public Performance and Broadcasting for Non-profit Purposes 50
1. Public Performance and Broadcasting of Works Already Made Public 50
2. Public Performance of Commercial Music Records or Cinematographic Works 50
H. Reproduction for Private Use 51
1. Statute 51
2. Indirect Infringement of Reproduction Right 51
3. Reproduction by Copying Apparatus in Public Use 53
4. Special Rules for Computer Program 53
I. Temporary Sound or Video Recordings by Broadcasting Service Providers 53
J. Exhibition or Reproduction of Works of Art, Etc. 53
K. Temporary Reproduction in Course of Using Works, Etc. 54
L. Fair Use of Copyrighted Work 54
III. Compulsory License of Copyrighted Work 54
A. Exploitation of Works Whose Holder of Author's Property Right Is Unknown 55

B. Broadcasting of Works Made Public 55
C. Production of Commercial Music Records 55

§8. Duration of Protection 55
I. Duration Period 55
II. Registration 56
A. Registration Office; Registrable Rights 56
B. Subjects to Register 56
1. Facts Relevant with Works 56
2. Facts Relevant with Rights 56
C. Submission of Copy 57
D. Reviewing Authority of Registration Office 57
E. Effects of Registration 57

§9. Neighbouring Rights 57
I. Holders of Neighbouring Rights 57
A. Performers 57
B. Sound Recording Producer 58
C. Broadcasting Service Provider 58
II. Substance of Neighbouring Rights 58
A. Performer's Neighbouring Rights 58
1. The Objects of Protection 58
2. Property Rights 58
3. Moral Rights 59
B. Sound Recording Producer's Neighbouring Rights 59
1. The Object of Protection 59
2. Property Rights 59
C. Broadcasting Service Provider's Neighbouring Rights 59
1. The Object of Protection 59
2. Property Rights 59
III. Limitations of Neighbouring Rights 63
IV. Relation between Copyright and Neighbouring Right 63

§10. Infringement and Remedies 63
I. Types of Infringement 63
A. Direct Infringement 63
B. Indirect Infringement 63
1. P2P Program Provider (*Soribada* Case) 64
2. Provider of Web-Hard Server 64
3. Portal Site Operator 64
4. Limitations of Responsibility for Online Service Provider 64
C. Act Deemed Infringement 65
1. Importation to Distribute 65
2. Possession of Infringing Articles to Distribute 65
3. Business Use of Illegal Copy of Computer Program 66
II. Protection of Technical Measures and Rights Management Information 66

A. Protection of Technical Protection Measures 66
B. Protection of Rights Management Information 66
III. Remedies 67
A. Prohibition Order (Injunction) 67
B. Damages 67
1. Presumption of Infringer's Profit to Damages 67
2. Reasonable Royalty 68
3. Presumption of Negligence for Infringement of Registered Works 68
4. Statutory Damages 68
5. Decision of Damages by Discretion 68
6. Comparative Negligence 69
C. Criminal Sanctions 69
D. Liability of Tort 69

§11. Overlapping and Relation to Other Intellectual Property Laws 69

Chapter 2. Patents 70

§1. Sources: Legislation 70

§2. Patentable Subject Matter 71
I. Inventions 71
A. Statutory Definition 71
B. 'Admitted' Types of Invention 71
II. Sorts of Inventions 72
A. Statutory Categories 72
B. Inventions of Theoretical Significance 72
1. New Use of Known Matter 72
2. Selection Inventions 73
3. Computer Program 73
4. Biotechnology 73
5. Business Method 74

§3. Conditions of Patentability 74
I. Substantial Conditions 74
A. Industrial Applicability 74
1. In General 74
2. Medical Skills (Surgery, Therapy, Diagnostic Methods, Etc.) 75
B. Novelty 76
1. Loss of Novelty 76
2. Non-prejudicial Disclosures: Inventions Not Considered Publicly Known 76
C. Enlarged Concept of Novelty 77
D. Inventive Step (Nonobviousness) 78

1. Method to Determine Inventive Step 78
2. Deciding Inventive Step for Special Types of Inventions 80

II. Specification 81

A. Claims 81

1. Sorts of Claims 81
2. Statutory Requirements in Claim Writing 82

B. Detail Description 83

1. Required Sufficiency and Method of Disclosure 83
2. Applicant's Duty to Report Arts Relevant with Invention 83
3. Disclosure of Producing Method and Utility for Material 84
4. Detail Descriptions for Special Types of Inventions 84

§4. FORMALITY (PROCEDURE FOR GRANT AND OBTAINING PATENT) 84

I. Principles Relevant to Patent Application 84

A. First to File 84
B. One Application for One Invention 85
C. Prohibition of New Matter Addition 85
D. Laying-Open of Application 85
E. Commencement of Examination under Request 86
F. Examination of 'Claim By Claim' and Rejection of Whole Claims 86

II. Amendment 86

A. Amendment in General 86
B. Divisional Application 86
C. Converted Application 87

III. Application with Priority Claim 87

A. Priority Claim under Treaty 87
B. Application with Domestic Priority Claim 87

§5. OWNERSHIP AND TRANSFER (ASSIGNMENT: LICENSES) 88

I. Right to Obtain Patent 88

A. Initial Entitlement of Right 88
B. Successor of Right 88

II. Derivation 88

A. Definition 88
B. Legal Effect of Derivation 88

III. Employee's Invention 89

A. Entitlement of Patent for Employee's Invention 89
B. Succession of Right by Employer 89
C. Calculation of Due Remuneration 90

IV. Establishment of Patent Right 90

V. Transfer 90

A. Transfer and Establishment of Pledge 90
B. License 91

1. Exclusive License 91
2. Non-exclusive License 91

§6. Scope of Exclusive Rights 91
I. Working of Patented Invention and All Elements Rule 91
II. Principles of Claim Interpretation 92
A. Literal Interpretation 92
B. Consideration of Detail Description 92
C. Consideration of Prosecution History 92
III. Substance of Exclusive Right of Patent 93

§7. Limitations and Exceptions to the Scope of Patent Protection: Compulsory License, Etc. 93
I. Statutory/Compulsory Licenses 93
A. Non-exclusive License for Prior User 93
B. Non-exclusive License for Business Based upon Double Patent 93
C. Compulsory Licenses 94
1. Expropriation of Patent Rights 94
2. Working of Patented Invention by Government, Etc. 94
3. Adjudication for Grant of Non-exclusive License 94
4. Trial for Granting Non-exclusive License 95
II. Limitations on Patent Rights: Experimental Use Etc. 95

§8. Duration of Protection: Maintaining and Termination of Patent Protection 96
I. Duration of Patent Right 96
II. Fees, Extinction, and Abandonment of Patent Right 96

§9. Infringement and Remedies 96
I. Infringements 96
A. Literal Infringement 97
B. Equivalent Infringement 97
1. Definition 97
2. Requirements 97
C. Infringement by Incremental Invention 98
D. Special Type of Incremental Invention: Selection Invention 99
E. Deeds Regarded as Infringement (Indirect Infringement) 99
1. Statute 99
2. Requirements to Constitute Indirect Infringement 100
3. Remedies for Indirect Infringement 101
II. Defences against Infringement Allegation 101
A. Invalidity of Patent 101
B. Arts in Public Domain 101
C. Unfair Competition 102
III. Remedies 102
A. Prohibition Order (Injunction) 102
B. Damages 103
1. 'Number of Transferred Articles by Infringer' X 'Profit per Unit of Right Holder' 103
2. Presumption of Infringer's Profit to Damages 103

3. Reasonable Royalty 104
4. Decision of Damages by Discretion 104
C. Return of Unjust Enrichment 104
D. Recovery of Reputation 104
E. Other Provisions to Support Damages Remuneration 105
1. Presumption of Process of Manufacturing 105
2. Presumption of Negligence 105
3. Submission Order of Documents 105
IV. Criminal Sanctions 105
V. Protection of Trade Secret in Patent Litigations 106

§10. Overlapping and Relation to Other Intellectual Property Laws 106

§11. Patent Trial and Patent Litigation 106
I. Patent Infringement Litigation 106
II. Patent Trial and Appeal to Patent Court 107
A. Patent Trials 107
1. Trial against Rejection to Application 107
2. Invalidation Trial 107
3. Trial to Confirm the Scope of Right 108
4. Trial for Correction 108
B. Appeal to Patent Court 108
C. Effects of Confirmed Trial Decision 108
D. Relation between Invalidation Trial and Infringement Suit 109

Chapter 3. Utility Models 110

§1. Sources: Legislation 110

§2. The Protection of Utility Models 110
I. Subject Matter 110
II. Patent Act Applied *Mutatis Mutandis* 111
III. Difference between Utility Model and Patent 111

Chapter 4. Trademarks 113

§1. Sources: Legislation 113

§2. Subject Matter of Protection 113
I. Trademark and Service Mark 113
II. Other Marks 114
A. Collective Mark 114
B. Geographical Collective Mark 114
C. Business Emblem 114
D. Certification Mark 115

III. Special Types of Symbols Eligible as Trademarks 115
IV. Trademark and Designated Goods 115
V. Registration 115

§3. CONDITIONS OF PROTECTION 116
I. Distinctiveness 116
A. Marks without Distinctiveness 116
1. Generic Term (TA Article 6(1) 1.) 116
2. A Trademark Used Customarily on the Goods (TA Article 6(1) 2.) 116
3. Descriptive Mark (TA Article 6(1) 3.) 116
4. Geographical Name (TA Article 6(1) 4.) 117
5. Popular Name (TA Article 6 (1) 5.) 117
6. A Trademark Consisting Solely of a Simple and Ordinary Mark (TA Article 6(1) 6.) 117
7. The Other Marks of Little Distinctiveness (TA Article 6(1) 7.) 117
B. Acquisition of Distinctiveness Through Continuous Use 117
C. Loss of Distinctiveness Through Continuous Use 118
II. Other Causes to Reject Registration 118
A. Marks Identical or Similar with National or International Emblems 118
B. Disparaging Marks Etc. (TA Article 7(1) 2.) 118
C. Mark Similar to the Symbol of Non-profit Public Entity (TA Article 7(1) 3.) 119
D. Mark against Public Order (TA Article 7(1) 4.) 119
E. Mark Similar with Emblem of Authorized Exhibition (TA Article 7(1) 5.) 119
F. Marks Mainly Consist of Well-Known Name of Others (TA Article 7(1) 6.) 119
G. Marks Confusingly Similar with Other's Mark (TA Article 7(1) 7, 9, 10.) 120
1. Mark Identical or Similar with Other's Mark Applied and Registered Priorly (TA Article 7(1) 7.) 120
2. Mark Identical or Similar with 'Well-Known' Mark of Others (TA Article 7(1) 9.) 120
3. Mark Possibly Causes Confusion with 'Very Well-Known' Mark of Others or Harm Distinctiveness (TA Article 7(1) 10.) 120
H. Deceptive Mark (TA Article 7(1) 11.) 121
1. Deception of Quality 121
2. Misleading Customers 121
I. Mark Filed under Unfair Purpose (TA Article 7(1) 12.) 121
J. Functional Marks (TA Article 7(1) 13.) 122
K. Geographical Origin of Wine and Spirits (TA Article 7(1) 14.) 122

§4. FORMALITIES (PROCEDURE FOR OBTAINING PROTECTION, ESTABLISHING AND MAINTAINING TRADEMARKS) 122
I. Application 122
A. In General 122
B. First to File 123
II. Examination and Public Review 123
III. Registration 123

§5. OWNERSHIP AND TRANSFER (ASSIGNMENT: LICENSES) 123
I. The Establishment and Transfer of Trademark 123
II. License 124

§6. SCOPE OF EXCLUSIVE RIGHTS 124

§7. LIMITATIONS OF THE SCOPE OF TRADEMARK PROTECTION 125
I. Statutory Limitations of Trademark Right 125
A. Trademark Same with User's Name 125
B. Descriptive Use 125
C. Name Customarily Used for Goods/Conspicuously Geographical Name 125
D. Functional Mark 126
II. Abuse of Trademark Right 126
A. Type of Unfair Competition Purpose 126
B. Type of Clear Invalidity 127
III. Prior User's Right 127
IV. Limitation from Copyright, Design Right of Others 127
V. Exhaustion 128

§8. USE REQUIREMENTS 128
I. Definition of 'Trademark Use' in Trademark Act 128
II. Non-use of Trademark 129
III. Trademark Use in Domain Name or Searching Keywords 129

§9. DURATION OF PROTECTION: RENEWAL – TERMINATION 130

§10. INFRINGEMENT AND REMEDIES 130
I. Infringement 130
A. Original Type of Infringement 130
B. Acts Deemed Infringement 130
C. Co-infringement of Trademark Infringement (Indirect Infringement) 131
II. Remedies 131
A. Prohibition Order (Injunction) 131
B. Damages 132
1. 'Number of Transferred Articles by Infringer' X 'Right Holder's Profit per Unit' 132
2. Presumption of Infringer's Profit to Damages 132

3. Reasonable Royalty 132
4. Decision of Damages by Discretion 133
5. Statutory Damages 133
6. Presumption of Wilfulness 133
III. Return of Unjust Enrichment 133
IV. Recovery of Reputation 134
V. Criminal Sanctions 134

§11. Overlapping and Relation to Other Intellectual Property 134

§12. Tribunals Relevant to Trademark Right 134
I. Trial against Rejection of Registration 134
II. Invalidation Trial 134
III. Trial to Confirm the Scope of Right 135
IV. Trial for Cancellation of Trademark Registration 135
A. Cancellation upon Inappropriate Use 135
B. Cancellation upon Non-use 136

Chapter 5. Trade Names 137

§1. Sources: Legislation 137

§2. The Protection of Trade Names 137

Chapter 6. Industrial Designs 139

§1. Source: Legislation 139

§2. Subject Matter of Protection 139
I. Design as Subject Matter 139
II. Requirement of Registration 139
A. Article 139
B. Shape, Pattern, and Colour 139
C. Aesthetic Impression in Visuality 139
III. Special Types of Design in Statute 140
A. Partial Design 140
B. Typeface 140
C. Design as a Set of Goods 140

§3. Conditions of Protection 140
I. General Conditions of Registration 140
A. Industrial Applicability 140
B. Novelty 141
1. General Rule 141
2. Non-prejudicial Disclosures 141
C. Nonobviousness 141

1. Obviousness from Known Design(s) 141
2. Obviousness from Conventional Design(s) 142
II. Negative Conditions 142

§4. FORMALITIES (PROCEDURE FOR GRANT AND OBTAINING PROTECTION) 142
I. General 142
II. Special Types of Applications in Statute 143
A. Relevant Design 143
B. Secret Design 143
C. Group Design 144
III. Specialties of Design Protection Act in Application and Examination 144
A. The Principle of Disclosure upon Request 144
B. Registration by Partial Examination 144
1. Definition 144
2. Post Grant Review 145

§5. OWNERSHIP AND TRANSFER (ASSIGNMENT: LICENSES) 145
I. Establishment and Transfer of Design Right 145
II. License 145

§6. SCOPE OF EXCLUSIVE RIGHTS 146

§7. LIMITATIONS OF THE SCOPE OF PROTECTION 146
I. Scope to Which Effect of Design Right Is Not Extended 146
II. Prior User's Right 147

§8. DURATION OF PROTECTION 147

§9. INFRINGEMENT AND REMEDIES 147
I. Infringement 147
A. Original Type of Infringement 147
B. Deeds Regarded as Infringement (Indirect Infringement) 148
II. Remedies 148
A. Prohibition Order (Injunction) 148
B. Damages 148
1. 'Number of Transferred Articles by Infringer X 'Right Holder's Profit per Unit' 149
2. Presumption of Infringer's Profit to Damages 149
3. Reasonable Royalty 149
4. Decision of Damages by Discretion 149
5. Presumption of Negligence 150
III. Return of Unjust Enrichment 150
IV. Recovery of Reputation 150
V. Criminal Sanctions 150

§10. Overlapping and Relation to Other Intellectual Property Law 151

§11. Trials Relevant to Design Right 151

Chapter 7. Plant Variety Protection 152

§1. Sources: Legislation 152

§2. Subject Matter of Protection 152

§3. Conditions of Protection 152
I. Novelty 152
II. Distinctness 152
III. Uniformity 153
IV. Stability 153
V. Denomination 153

§4. Formalities (Procedure for Grant and Obtaining Protection) 153
I. Application 153
II. Examination 154
III. Provisional Protection 154
IV. Decision of Registration 154

§5. Ownership and Transfer (Assignment: Licenses) 154
I. Assignment 154
II. License 155

§6. Scope of Exclusive Rights 155

§7. Limitations of the Scope of Protection 156
I. Scope to Which Effect of Breeder's Right Is Not Extended 156
II. Exhaustion 156

§ 8. Duration of Protection 156

§9. Infringement and Remedies 156
I. Prohibition Order (Injunction) 156
II. Acts Deemed Infringement 156
III. Damages 157
IV. Recovery of Reputation 157
V. Criminal Sanctions 157

§10. Overlapping and Relation to Other Intellectual Property Laws 157

§11. Trials Relevant to Breeder's Right 157

Chapter 8. Chip Protection 158

§1. SOURCES: LEGISLATION 158

§2. SUBJECT MATTER OF PROTECTION 158

§3. CONDITIONS OF PROTECTION 158

§4. FORMALITIES (PROCEDURE FOR GRANT AND OBTAINING PROTECTION) 158
I. Application for Registration 158
II. Rejection of Applications 159
III. Registration of Creation and Public Notices 159
IV. Cancellation of Registered Rights 159

§5. OWNERSHIP AND TRANSFER (ASSIGNMENT: LICENSES) 159
I. Establishment and Assignment 159
II. License 160
A. Exclusive License 160
B. Non-exclusive License 160

§6. SCOPE OF EXCLUSIVE RIGHTS 160

§7. LIMITATIONS OF THE SCOPE OF PROTECTION 161
I. Limitations of Scope of Layout-Design Rights 161
II. Exhaustion 161
III. Immunity for Bona Fide Person 161
IV. Adjudication on Non-exclusive License Grant 161

§8. DURATION OF PROTECTION 161

§9. INFRINGEMENT AND REMEDIES 162
I. Prohibition Order (Injunction) 162
II. Damages 162
A. General 162
B. Presumption of Infringer's Profit as Damages 162
C. Reasonable Royalty 162
III. Unauthorized User's Duty of Compensation for the Use Prior to Registration 162

§10. OVERLAPPING AND RELATION TO OTHER INTELLECTUAL PROPERTY LAWS 163

Chapter 9. Trade Secrets/Confidential Information 164

§1. SOURCES: LEGISLATION 164

§2. THE PROTECTION OF TRADE SECRETS/CONFIDENTIAL INFORMATION 164
I. Definition of Trade Secret 164
II. Categories of Trade Secret Infringement 165
A. Lineage of Unfair 'Acquirement' 165
1. Unfair Acquirement, Use, and Disclosure of Trade Secret 165
2. Subsequent Acquirement, Use, Disclosure of Unfairly Acquired Trade Secret 165
3. Use or Disclosure of Trade Secret after Acquirement in Good Faith 165
B. Lineage of Unfair 'Disclosure' 165
1. Unfair Disclosure of Trade Secret 165
2. The Acquirement, Use, or Disclosure of Unfairly Disclosed Trade Secret 166
3. Use or Disclosure of Trade Secret after Acquirement in Good faith 166
III. Remedies for Infringement 166
A. Prohibition Order (Injunction) 166
B. Damages Etc. 166
C. Special Rule for Infringement in Good Faith 167
IV. Criminal Sanctions 167

Chapter 10. Geographical Indications and Appellations of Origin 168

Chapter 11. Unfair Competition 169

§1. SOURCES: LEGISLATION 169

§2. RULES OF UNFAIR COMPETITION 169
I. Statutory Types of Unfair Competition 169
A. To Arouse Confusion with Other's Goods or Business 169
1. Deeds to Confuse Source Identity of Goods 169
2. Deeds to Cause Confusion with Another Person's Business 170
B. To Damage Distinctiveness or Reputation of Prominent Identification 170
C. Other Types of Unfair Competition Deeds in Statute 171
1. False Indication About Origin Place 171
2. Arousing Public Confusion About Place of Production or Process 171
3. Arousing Misconception About Quality of Goods Etc. 171
4. Unjustifiable Use of Mark by Agent 172
5. Domain Name Registration in Unjust Purpose 172
6. Copying the Figure of Other's Goods 173
II. Supplementary Types of Unfair Competition Deeds 173

§3. Remedies 173
I. Prohibition Order (Injunction) 173
II. Damages 174
A. 'Number of Transferred Articles by Infringer' X 'Right Holder's Profit per Unit' 174
B. Presumption of Infringer's Profit to Damages 174
C. Reasonable Royalty 175
D. Decision of Damages by Discretion 175
III. Return of Unjust Enrichment 175
IV. Recovery of Reputation 175
V. Criminal Sanctions 175

Selected Bibliography 177

Index 181

List of Abbreviations

Art.	Article
CA	Copyright Act
DA	Design Protection Act
IMF	International Monetary Fund
OECD	Organisation for Economic Cooperation and Development
NVPPA	New Varieties of Plants Protection Act
PA	Patent Act
TA	Trademark Act
Sct.	Supreme Court of Korea
WIPO	World Intellectual Property Organization
KIPO	Korean Intellectual Property Office

List of Abbreviations

General Introduction

§1. General Background

I. Geography

1. Location: The Republic of Korea (South Korea) is on Korean peninsula in Far East Asia. Its width is 99,720 Km^2 (world's 109th).

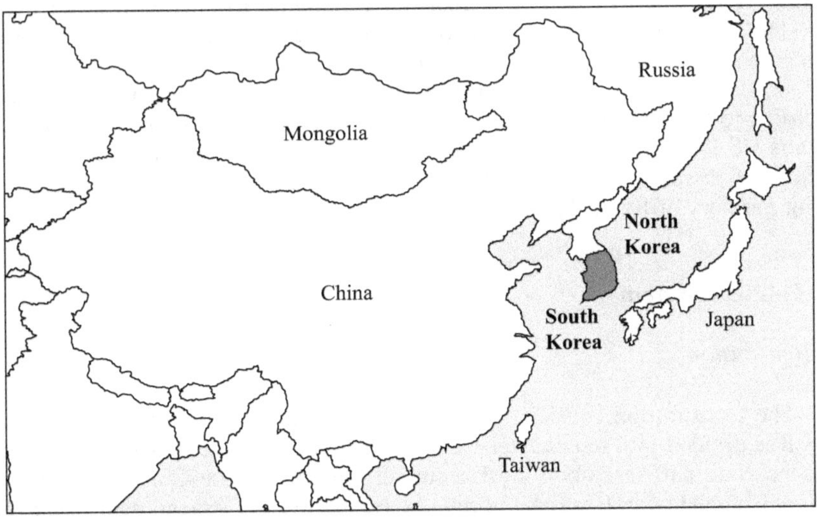

Geographically, Korea is located between China and Japan. Since 1945, South Korea has been divided from North Korea, which is a communist sovereign. Two parties suffered Korean War (1950–1953) when the world passed through 'Cold War' era of ideological enmity.

2. Administrative Divisions: South Korea has one special city, nine provinces, six metropolitan cities, and one special self-governing city:

- Special city (Capital): Seoul.
- Provinces: Gyeonggi, Gangwon, Chungbuk, Chungnam, Gyeongbuk, Gyeongnam, Jeonbuk, Jeonnam, and Jeju.

– Metropolitan cities: Busan, Incheon, Daegu, Daejeon, Gwangju, and Ulsan.
– Special self-governing city: Sejong.

II. Cultural Background

3. People: The population of South Korea is 49 million (July 2014 est.) and 9.778 million of them reside in Seoul, the capital city of South Korea. The populations of other major cities are: Busan (3.5 million), Incheon (2.8 million), Daegu (2.5 million), Daejeon (1.5 million), Gwangju (1.5 million), and Ulsan (1.1 million) (2012).

4. Language: The language is 'Korean' and Korea has its own alphabet ('Hangeul'). In addition, English is widely taught to students in every level of education.

5. Economic status: South Korea is currently the world's 12th largest economy and is a Member State of Organisation for Economic Cooperation and Development (OECD). South Korea has demonstrated huge growth and global integration to become a high-tech industrialized economy. Its semiconductor, automobile, shipbuilding, steel making, and IT industries are on the leading edge in global markets. According to International Monetary Fund (IMF) estimation in 2013, GDP of South Korea is US Dollar (USD) 198 trillion (15th of global ranking) and per capita GNI is USD 23,837 (33rd of global ranking). China, the US, and Japan are three biggest trading partners of South Korea.

III. Political System

A. *Constitution*

6. The Constitution consists of a preamble, 130 articles, and six supplementary rules. It is divided into ten chapters: General Provisions, Rights and Duties of Citizens, the National Assembly, the Executive, the Courts, the Constitutional Court, Election Management, Local Authority, the Economy, and Amendments to the Constitution. The basic principles of the Korean Constitution include the sovereignty of the people, division of powers, the pursuit of peaceful and democratic unification of South and North Korea, the pursuit of international peace and cooperation, the rule of law and the responsibility of the State to promote welfare.

B. *Division of Power*

1. Legislative Branch

7. Legislative power is vested in the National Assembly, a unicameral legislature. Among the functions of National Assembly, the foremost is making laws.

Other major functions of the Assembly are approval of the national budget, inspecting or investigating specific matters of State affairs and impeachment. National Assembly is composed of 300 members serving four-year terms. Among 300 members, 246 are elected by popular vote from local constituencies, and the remaining fifty-four members are qualified through a proportional representation system in which seats are allocated to each political party that has gained 3% or more of all valid votes or five or more seats in the local constituency election.

2. Executive Branch (President and Cabinet)

8. The president plays five main roles under constitution as: (1) the head of State symbolizing and representing the entire nation, (2) the chief administrator and head of cabinet to enforce the laws and to issue orders and decrees, (3) the chief policy maker and a key lawmaker to propose legislative bills to the National Assembly or express views to the legislature, (4) the commander-in-chief of the armed forces, and (5) nation's top diplomat and foreign policy maker. The cabinet is made up of fifteen to thirty members and presided over by the President. The Prime Minister, the principal executive assistant to the President is appointed by the President and approved by National Assembly. The Prime Minister supervises the administrative ministries of the cabinet and manages the policy coordination under the direction of the President. Members of the Cabinet are appointed by the President upon recommendation by the Prime Minister.

3. Judiciary

9. Judicial Independence: Article 103 of Constitution promulgates judicial independence stipulating that judges should only follow the Constitution, law and regulation and conscience. It articulates that no judge is subject to involuntary dismissal from office except by an impeachment or a sentence of imprisonment or heavier. Further, a judge cannot be subject to suspension from office, to a reduction of salaries or to unfavourable treatments except by disciplinary measures.

Structure: The Judiciary of Korea consists of the Supreme Court, High Courts, District Courts, and special courts such as Patent Court, Family Court, and Administrative Court. The Constitution separately vests The Constitutional Court with powers to judge constitutional issues such as the constitutionality of a law, impeachment, dissolution of a political party, constitutional petitions filed directly to the Constitutional Court, and jurisdictional conflicts involving State agencies and/or local governments.

§2. Judicial System

I. Legal System and Jurisdictions of Courts

10. The Legal System of South Korea is heavily influenced by continental European civil law systems, while the mixtures of Anglo-American law elements are also found partly. In principle, Korean judiciary follows three instance systems, which has tiers of District Courts, High Courts, and the Supreme Court.

The Supreme Court is the highest judicial tier. It hears appeals on cases rendered by lower courts. High Courts hear appealed cases rendered by district, administrative and family courts. There are High Courts of local jurisdictions in five major cities (Seoul, Busan, Daegu, Daejon, and Gwangju). The Patent Court reviews decisions rendered by the patent office (Korean Intellectual Property Office: hereinafter, referred as KIPO). The Patent Court is positioned on the same level as the high court.

District Courts are located in Seoul and in thirteen local cities. The District courts exercise first instance jurisdictions over civil, criminal, administrative, electoral, and other judicial matters. They shall also exercise the power to administer and supervise extra-judicial matters such as immovable and movable property registration, corporation registration, family registration, deposit, and the duties of marshal. The Family Court is empowered to hear all cases involving matrimonial, juvenile, or other domestic matters. The Administrative Court handles administrative cases only.

II. Appointment of Judges

11. The Chief Justice of the Supreme Court is appointed by the President with the consent of the National Assembly. Other justices are appointed by the President upon the recommendation of the Chief Justice. The term of office for the Chief Justice is six years and is not renewable. The judges of High Court and lower courts are appointed by the Chief Justice of Supreme Court. With regard to the appointment rule, Korea is under reformation. From the establishment of modern legal system in 1948, the judges have been appointed among the candidates who passed 'National Judicial Examination,' which admits highly limited numbers and the Supreme Court provided them with intensive legal discipline course for judicial practice. However, with the institution of 'Law School System' as from 2009, Korea is moving toward the paradigm to appoint judges among 'careered lawyers' in various field of practice. Both system are estimated to have merits and flaws altogether. As the transition of system is in its initial stage, most current judges in Korea are appointed under old system yet. As of December 2012, the number of judges in Korea is 2,739.

III. Proceedings

A. Civil Proceedings

12. Civil proceedings begin when a plaintiff files a complaint to a district court. When the complaint is filed, the court serves the defendant with a duplicate and requires him/her to file a written answer within thirty days. If the defendant fails to file a written answer within such time limit, the court may render a judgment without hearings. If the defendant submits a written answer, the court holds the pleading process and the hearings, and then renders a judgment. In pleading process, both parties enter an offence and defence on allegations and evidence in writing. In hearing, both parties clarify their positions on disputed issues as well as to examine witnesses before the court. The losing party who is dissatisfied with the judgment can appeal within two weeks from the date the judgment is served.

B. Criminal Proceedings

13. Criminal proceedings begin when a public prosecutor institutes a criminal action. The public prosecutor may bring a case before the court by summary proceedings when it is deemed that the offence is punishable by fine. In such a case, the judge usually issues the summary order without holding a trial. Generally, Korea has no jury trial system, while the jury trial is available for limited sorts of felonies upon request of the accused. The jury verdict has only advisory effect to judges. In procedure, the prosecutor introduces evidence to the court, questions the defendant, examines the witness, and performs other procedural duties. The accused is entitled to be assisted by the counsel for his/her defence in the course of investigation as well as trial proceedings. It is mandated that the court appoints a defence counsel when the defendant is a minor, 70 years or older, suspected of mental illness, or cannot afford a counsel. In criminal proceedings, it lies upon the public prosecutor to prove guilt of the accused. When a confession by the accused is the only evidence against him/her, he/she cannot be judged guilty. Corroborating evidence in support of a confession is indispensable for conviction. After the hearing process, the judge renders final judgment on whether the defendant is guilty of a crime; and, if so, how severe the sentence should be. If guilt has not been proved beyond a reasonable doubt, the court declares the accused not guilty. Not only the accused but also the public prosecutor can bring an appeal against the judgment rendered by the trial court within seven days from the date the judgment is rendered.

IV. Judicial Process of Intellectual Property Right Dispute

14. Judicial process relevant to intellectual property right has 'bifurcated' features in Korea. First, the industrial intellectual property rights e.g., patent, trademark, design, and ant plant variety, have their own judicial tracks beginning at KIPO tribunal and continued in Patent Court and Supreme Court. Such process covers, grant of right, in rem invalidation of granted right, confirmation of the scope of right, etc. Second, the remedies from infringement of any intellectual property right (including copyright and said industrial intellectual property rights) is adjudicated by civil court, as it has nature of 'tort' in Civil Act. The brief introduction of former judicial track is like the followings.

A. Tribunal in KIPO (Korean Intellectual Property Office)

15. For industrial intellectual property such as patent, trademark and industrial design for which registration is to be entailed, KIPO tribunal has first instance jurisdiction for statutory types of trial cases. The tribunal's decision is appealed to the Patent Court, and finally to the Supreme Court. The primary trials that tribunal board of KIPO deals with are like the following:

16.

(1) Appealing Trial against Rejection to Application:[1] When an applicant has received a decision of rejection or revocation from an examiner, that person may demand an appeal within thirty days as from the date he/she received the rejection notice.
(2) Invalidation Trial:[2] Any interested party or examiner may request an invalidation trial against registered patent, trademark, or design. Causes of invalidation are listed in each Act restrictively.
(3) Trial to confirm the scope of right:[3] A right holder may request the trial to confirm that a certain type of third party's work is within the scope of his/her right constituting infringement. The third party may also initiate trial to request decision that his/her work is out of registered right's scope.
(4) Trial for Correction:[4] A patent right holder may demand a trial for corrections of specifications or drawings to evade invalidation of his/her patent. The correction is allowable only to narrow a claim; to correct a clerical error; to clarify an ambiguous description.

B. Appeal to Patent Court

17. The losing party in tribunal may appeal to the Patent Court. The cases are ruled by the panels of three judges. In patent and utility model cases, in-house technical advisor provides presentation on technical issues for judges' better understanding. As civil litigation, the principles of oral proceedings, burden of pleading, and proof apply to patent court's proceedings too. Patent attorneys, in addition to lawyers, are permitted to represent the parties in the Patent Court, while not allowed for infringement litigations. A discussion is in progress recently on whether patent attorneys should be allowed to represent the parities in infringement litigations also. Any appeal of the Patent Court's decisions should be brought directly to the Supreme Court, as the Patent Court is an appellate-level court.

C. Infringement Suit

18. While the Patent Court exercises exclusive appellate jurisdiction over aforementioned KIPO tribunal decisions, the infringement cases, where litigants seek for relieves by means of damages, injunctions of restitution of commercial credit, are

1. Patent Act (Hereinafter, PA) Art. 132-3; Trademark Act (Hereinafter, TA) Art. 70-2; Design Protection Act (Hereinafter, DA) Art. 120.
2. PA Art. 133; TA Art. 71; DA Art. 121.
3. PA Art. 135; TA Art. 75; DA Art. 122.
4. PA Art. 136.

referred to ordinary courts under their respective civil jurisdiction. As of an en banc decision of Supreme Court in 2012,[5] the defendant in infringement suit may argue the validity of registered patent or trademark by means of defence on 'any' ground (including obviousness of patented invention). Before said en banc decision, the courts had dismissed defendant's allegation of invalidity against registered patent or trademark as long as it had not been definitely nullified through invalidation trial process.

5. Supreme Court (Hereinafter, abbreviated as Sct.) en banc, 2012. 1. 19. – 2010 Da 95390.

Chapter 1. Copyright and Neighbouring Rights

§1. SOURCES: LEGISLATION

19. As South Korea is a continental law-system country, statutes are the sources of law. As for copyright, the Copyright Act is main source of law. Subordinately, Presidential Decree and Enforcement Rule in hierarchy regulate copyrights and other relevant rights. Copyright Act of Korea was initially enacted on 28 January 1957 (Act No. 432) and has been amended twenty-two times to current version of 17 October 2013 (Act No. 11903). Particularly important amendments among them are as the followings:[6]

- 1 July 1987 (Act No. 3916): adoption of neighbouring right, reciprocity for foreigner's work, attributing copyright of employee's work to employer
- 1 July 1994 (Act No. 4717): extension of neighbouring right's protection period from twenty years to fifty years, protection of Data Base as a compilation work, adoption of Rental Right for phonorecords
- 1 July 1996 (Act No. 5015): reflection of World Trade Organization (WTO) agreement, retroactive protection of foreign works published prior to enforcement date of treaty
- 1 July 2000 (Act No. 6134): adopting Right of Public Transmission as a property right
- 1 July 2003 (Act No. 6881): providing, immunity of responsibility for Online Service Provider; prohibition of technical protection measures incapacitation
- 23 July 2009 (Act No. 9625): merger of Computer Program Protection Act into Copyright Act
- 1 July 2011 (Act No. 10807): reflecting KOR-US FTA: extension of copyright protection period to seventy years after author's death
- 15 March 2012 (Act No. 11110): reflection of KOR-US FTA: stipulation of temporary copying as a type of copying; adoption of general fair use rule.

20. On the other hand, as the treaties signed and promulgated under Constitution and generally accepted international rules of law have same effect with domestic law (Constitution Article 6(1)), copyright treaties also becomes effective sources of law. Upon this rule, Copyright Act stipulates that foreigners' works shall be protected in accordance with the treaties, which Korea has acceded to or concluded.[7] The important copyright-related treaties Korea joined and the dates they came into force are as the following (date of establishment: date of force in Korea):

- The Berne Convention for the Protection of Literary and Artistic Works (1886: 1996).
- The Universal Copyright Convention (UCC) (1952: 1987).

6. Effective dates other than revision dates are indicated.
7. Copyright Act (Hereinafter, CA) Art. 3(1).

- Rome Convention for the Protection of Performers, Producers of Phonograms and Broadcasting Organizations (1961: 2009).
- TRIPs (1994: 1995).
- The World Intellectual Property Organization Copyright Treaty (1996: 2004).
- The WIPO Performances and Phonograms Treaty (1996: 2009).

Though the treaties are separate sources of law for Copyright issues, it is rare that a provision of treaty is directly applied to individual case in Korea as National Assembly has been reflecting the substance of the treaties into Copyright Act through repetitive amendments.[8]

§2. Subject Matter of Protection

I. Works

21. Subject matter of copyright protection is 'works'. Copyright Act defines works as creative productions in which human ideas or emotions are expressed[9] and 'authors' as the persons who create works.[10] Copyright Act Article 4(1) enumerates the types of works to be protected as the following, which are not limiting but exemplifying. Any other types of works are protectable under Copyright Act as long as it is creative productions in which human ideas or emotions are expressed:

(1) Novels, poems, theses, lectures, speeches, plays, and other literary works.
(2) Musical works.
(3) Theatrical works including dramas, choreographies, pantomimes, and other theatrical works.
(4) Paintings, calligraphic works, sculptures, prints, crafts, works of applied art, and other artistic works.
(5) Architecture, architectural models, architectural plans, and other architectural works.
(6) Photographic works (including other works produced by similar methods).
(7) Cinematographic works.
(8) Maps, charts, plans, sketches, models, and other diagrammatic works.
(9) Computer program works.

22. Certain types of non-copyrightable works are protected under copyright law. Namely, some non-copyrightable works and legal issues pertaining to them are incorporated into copyright law's regulation. It is because the Copyright Act protects performers, producers of phonograms, and broadcasting organizations as 'neighbours' and their works include non-copyrightable works as well as copyrightable works. The definition clause of Copyright Act reflects this idea. For example,

8. As for the case that the provision of treaty was directly applied to foreign litigation party, refer to Seoul Central District Court, 2008. 6. 20 – 2007 Gahap 43936.
9. CA. Art. 2.1.
10. CA. Art. 2.2.

Article 2.4 defines 'performers' as persons who express works by acting, dancing, musical playing, singing, narrating, reciting, or other artistic means, or who express 'something other than the works' by a similar method. Article 2.5 defines 'phonogram' as media in which the 'sound' is fixed. It does not limit the contents of sound to copyrightable works. Article 2.8 defines 'broadcasting' as any transmission of sounds, images, or sounds and images intended for simultaneous reception by the public. It does not limit the contents of broadcasting as copyrightable works. Article 2.19 defines 'database' as compilation that arranges or composes subject matters systematically so that one can individually access or search such subject matters. It does not limit the contents of database as copyrightable works.

II. Works Excluded From Protection

A. *Governmental Works*[11]

23. Governmental works excluded from protection are:

(1) Constitution, laws, treaties, decrees, ordinances, and rules.
(2) Notices, public notifications, directions, and others similar to them issued by the national or local government.
(3) Judgments, decisions, orders, or rulings of courts, as well as rulings and decisions made by the administrative appeal procedures or other similar procedures.
(4) Compilations or translations of works as referred to in (1) to (3), which are produced by the national or local government.

B. *Current News Reports Transmitting Simple Facts*[12]

24. Simple delivery of topical coverage is not protected by copyright. However, this rule is applicable only to the facts or information that media portrays with typical and concise writing format (e.g., sports news, weather forecast, report of trial, or investigation etc.). The contents more than short and simple description of fact does not belong to the exceptions here.

C. *Program Language, Protocol, and Solutions*[13]

25. Copyright Act shall not apply to the following matters used to prepare programs:

(1) Programming language: characters, symbols, and their systems as means for expressing programs.

11. CA. Art. 7.
12. CA. Art. 5.
13. CA. Art. 101-2.

(2) Protocol: a special agreement on how to use programming language in a specific program.
(3) Solutions: combination methods of instructions and commands in a program.

These generally belong to the realm of ideas. Given regarded as expressions, they have nature as basic measures in computer programming, which should be available to anyone for his/her creation in such field.

III. Special Categories of Works

A. *Special Subjects Listed in Copyright Act*

1. Derivative Work

26. Derivative work means a creative work produced by means of translation, arrangement, alteration, dramatization, cinematization, etc., of an original work. To be deemed derivative work, the work should be upon original work maintaining certain degree of similarity, while the alteration is substantial enough to show its own creativity from derived work. Therefore, the junior work of simple modification lacking its own creativity cannot be entitled to copyright protection as derivative work.[14] Derivative work is protected as an independent work.[15] However, the protection of a derivative work shall not affect original copyright,[16] limiting the scope of derivative work's right to incremental creativity it generated.[17] In addition, the junior worker enjoys right for derivative work whether or not he obtained permission from original copyright holder.[18] For instance, if a third party publishes translated version of novel without translator's consent, it is infringement of translator's copyright whether the translation is made under original author's permission or not. Therefore, the publisher needs permission from both parties: author and translator, as the published work contains every portion of both works. In the aspect between translator and author, translating a novel without author's consent constitutes infringement of author's right to make derivative work.

2. Compilation Work

27. The term 'compilation works' means the compiled matters which are of creative nature in terms of selection, arrangement or composition of their subject matters.[19] The creativity of compilation work is about the selection and rearrangement

14. SCt. 2012. 2. 23 – 2010 Da 66637.
15. CA. Art. 5(1).
16. CA. Art. 5(2).
17. SCt. 2010. 11. 11 – 2009 Da 16742.
18. SCt. 2004. 9. 24 – 2002 Da 45895.
19. CA. Art. 2.18.

of pre-existing materials. Whether compilation is made under permission of original works' right holder does not affect the subsistence of this right.[20] Just as derivative works, compilation work is protected independently but its scope does not extend to its contents.[21] Hence, a third party to use compilation work must get permission not only from compilation works' right holder but also from original works' right holders.

3. Cinematographic Work

28. Due to the nature that a large number of the copyright and neighbouring right holders are involved in film-making, it is necessary to dispose and simplify relevant rights in advance in order to avoid conflict among right holders and capacitate proper exploitation. Copyright Act provides several presumption rules as followings to manage entanglement of copyrights and neighbouring rights. The articles have only presumptive effects and parties may contract otherwise:

(1) Between copyright holders and producer:[22] If the holder of author's property right permits another person to exploit his/her works by means of cinematization, such permission shall be presumed to include the following rights, unless otherwise expressly stipulated:
   - To dramatize a work for the production of a cinematographic work.
   - To publicly present a cinematographic work aiming at a public presentation.
   - To broadcast a cinematographic work aiming at a broadcasting.
   - To transmit a cinematographic work aiming at a transmission on the internet.
   - To reproduce and distribute a cinematographic work for its original purpose.
   - To exploit the translation of a cinematographic work in the same manner as the cinematographic work.

   If the copyright holder permits a person to exploit his/her work by means of cinematization, he/she may permit, after the lapse of five years from the date of his/her permission, the cinematization of the work in another form of cinematographic work.
(2) Between co-operators and producer:[23] Where a producer of a cinematographic work and co-operator have obtained a copyright to cinematographic work, the rights necessary to exploit such work shall be presumed to have been transferred to the producer, whereas the copyright of a novel, play, work of art, or musical work used for the work shall not be affected by former presumption. The performer's right of, reproduction (Article 69); distribution (Article 70); broadcasting (Article 73) and public transmission (Article 74) shall be presumed to have been transferred to the producer.

20. SCt. 1996. 12. 6 – 96 Do 2440.
21. CA. Art. 6.
22. CA. Art. 99.
23. CA. Art. 100.

B. *Special Subjects of Theoretical Matters*

1. Applied Arts

29. The term 'works of applied art' means the artistic works that may be copied on the goods in the same shapes, and whose originality may be recognized apart from the relevant applied goods, and that include designs, etc.[24] As stipulated in the article, Copyright Act renders overlapped protection to design. Namely, industrial design is also covered by Design Protection Act, while it is a subject matter of copyright protection in the name of 'applied art'. Before relevant article of Copyright Act was amended as current version, Supreme Court articulated that the applied arts are protected by only Design Protection Act; the 'outstanding artistic value' is required for them to be protected by Copyright Act. The Supreme Court changed its attitude after Copyright Act's amendment and allows double protection as applied art.[25] In the course of obtaining right, copyright does not entail any formality other than creation, while design protection requires examination and registration. Duration periods of each right also differs: author's lifetime and seventy years after death for copyright, twenty years after filing date for design.

2. Computer Program

30. Initially, computer program was protected by sui generis law of Computer Program Protection Act, which has been merged into Copyright Act since 2009. It is to be noted that:

(1) Computer program may be also registered as patent once it meets statutory requisites of Patent Act.
(2) Limitations for property right of computer program are stipulated separately from those of copyright.[26]
(3) The continued use of infringing computer program is deemed fair once the user obtained such program in good faith.[27]
(4) The author of commercial computer program is endowed with Rental Right.[28]

3. Database

31. The producer of Database is protected under Copyright Act even where he/she is neither a copyright nor neighbouring right holder. Right of reproduction, public transmission, broadcasting, and distribution are rendered to the database

24. CA. Art. 2. 15.
25. SCt. 2004. 7. 22. – 2003 Do 7572.
26. CA. Art. 37-2; Art. 101-3.
27. CA. Art. 124. 3.
28. CA. Art. 21.

producer.[29] The rights of database producer begin to exist when database is completed, and continues for five years as from the first day of next year.[30]

4. Character

32. Majority of commentators take literary character as close to idea than expression, disqualifying independent copyright protection. Meanwhile, Supreme Court promulgates creative characters in comic books, television, movies, newspapers, magazines, etc., which are visually depicted and exposed to public, are subject to independent copyright.[31]

5. Works against Order of Public

33. Whether the contents of work are against social order is distinguished from its copyrightability. Supreme Court remarks, 'Copyright hinge only on whether it is creative expression of human thoughts or emotions and its morality does not count. Therefore, the immoral or even illegal contents of a work do not encumber its copyrightability.'[32]

§3. Conditions of Protection

I. Formal Requirements

34. Copyrightable works are under protection from the very moment or creation and no additional condition such as fixation is required. Copyright registration is not the requisite of protection at all, whereas registration gives presumption of validity for the work and constructive notice of right to the third party.

II. Creativity

A. *Substance of Creativity Requirement*

35. The work needs to meet creativity standard to enjoy copyright protection. Creativity here denotes that the work must not be a simple duplication of preexisting work of others (originality), and have a minimum degree amount of creative merit (creativity in narrow meaning). Courts adjure 'originality' and 'creativity in narrow meaning' for a work to be protected under Copyright Act.[33]

29. CA. Art. 93.
30. CA. Art. 95.
31. SCt. 2003. 10. 23 – 2002 Do 446.
32. SCt. 1990. 10. 23 – 90 Daka 8845.
33. SCt. 1997. 11. 25 – 97 Do 2227 et al.

B. Creativity in Functional Works

36. Large portion of cases that adjudicated destitution of creativity lies with functional works. Courts reason that:

> Generally, functional works such as construction design drawings; maps; document formats are heavily oriented to transmission of practical idea than artistic expression. The alternatives of expressions are limited due to standard; efficiency; necessity of brevity etc. The creativity of such expressions shall be estimated low letting others express their idea free without concern of copyright infringement.[34]

C. De Facto Standard and Creativity

37. A lower court denied copyright protection against a user interface software which was so widely used in public and became a 'de facto standard', for which other's alternative to express same idea in different way became limited.[35] Once a user interface introduced by first-comer is so widely used by public changing the nature into a functional element, it is inappropriate to protect it by copyright, driving public to pay perpetual royalty or to use different interface. The latter forces public to endure inconvenience of learning new interface, which is obviously a social waste.

D. Scènes à Faire and Creativity

38. Supreme Court adjudicated a '*scènes à faire*': typical expressional elements in novels or movies to depict a character or topic, is rather in the realm of idea to divesture copyright protection.[36]

§4. OWNERSHIP

I. General Rule

39. In accordance with Berne Convention, Korea follows 'Non-formality Rule' for existence and attribution of copyright. Thus copyright subsists from the very moment of creation of work and belongs to the creator.

34. SCt. 2005. 1. 27. – 2002 Do 965.
35. Seoul High Court, 2008. 6. 10 – 2007 Na 58805.
36. SCt. 2000. 10. 24 – 99 Da 10813.

II. Joint Authorship

A. *Conditions of Joint Authorship*

40. The term 'joint work' means a work jointly created by two or more persons, and the portion of respective contribution may not be utilized by taking it apart.[37] To be a joint work, multiple entities must be involved in creative expression[38] and the joint work shall be made under intention of co-operation.

B. *Effect of Joint Authorship*

41. Author's moral right to a joint work may not be exercised without the unanimous agreement of all the authors concerned. In such cases, each of the authors may not, in bad faith, prevent the agreement from being reached.[39]

Author's property right to a joint work may not be exercised without the unanimous agreement of all holders, and no holder of right shall be entitled to assign or pledge his/her share without unanimous consent of right holders. In such cases, each holder may not prevent the agreement in bad faith.[40] The profit accrued from the exploitation of a joint work shall be apportioned among authors according to the degrees of contribution by each author, unless otherwise stipulated. In such cases, if the degree of each contribution is not clear, the profit may be equally apportioned to all the authors.[41] The reason to require unanimous agreement in transfer of share is that joint authors' interests are seriously annexed to who becomes new share holder: (1) as it is often the case that market value of a work is depreciated once the contents are marketed by a member, and (2) as the member exercises privilege of agreement and bears duty to account benefits to whole members.

III. Employee's Work

A. *Definition*

42. The term 'employee's work' means a work made out professionally by a person engaged in the duty of employee according to the plan of the employer.[42]

B. *Ownership of Copyright for Employee's Work*

43. When an employee's work is made public in the name of employer, the authorship goes to employer.[43] This contrasts to the general norm that the right for

37. CA. Art. 2. 21.
38. SCt. 2009. 12. 10 – 2007 Do 7181.
39. CA. Art. 15(1).
40. CA. Art. 48(1).
41. CA. Art. 48(2).
42. CA. Art 2. 31.
43. CA. Art. 9.

employee's invention or design belongs to the employee, while the royalty free license is conferred on the employer for such invention or design. It is hard for transaction partner to acknowledge if a work is employee's work or not. Thus, statutorily concentrating copyright to the employer assures legal stability and invigorates transactions of work. This rule is further transformed for preference of employers in software; the element of 'publication in the name of employer' is unrequested for attribution. Meanwhile, provided that a work is made not by employment but by independent contract/ commission, copyright of such work is attributed to creator and the conditions of, use, transfer, payment are decided by party's agreement.

§5. Transfer

I. Assignment

44. Author's property right may be assigned or pledged in whole or in part. Such transfer shall not bind third parties without registration.[44] Thus, when the author transfers identical property right to multiple parties, the one that registers transfer has dominating position regardless of the timing of contract. Where author's property right is transferred by assignment in whole, the right of the production and use of a derivative work shall be presumed not to be included in the transfer. In cases of a computer program, the right of production of a derivative work shall be presumed to have been transferred together unless otherwise stipulated.[45] Thus, in principal, the author still enjoys the right to make derivative work once he transferred property right of original work. This means that the third party who makes derivative work has to get permission not from transferee but from transferor and even the transferee himself cannot make derivative work without consent of transferor.

II. License

45. The property right of copyright can be licensed. License may be given either in exclusive or non-exclusive manner through contract. Copyright Act also provides 'Exclusive Publication License', which has exclusivity.[46] Such license is available only for the property rights of reproduction and internet transmission. To enjoy the exclusivity against third party, the license is required to be registered.[47] The registered licensee of this type may enforce the right by demanding injunction and damages in his/her name. Until the Copyright Act amendment of 2011, there had been no third-party effective license but Publishing Right. Publishing Right is a conventional right endowed to the book publisher, which enables the publisher to claim exclusive right to reproduce and distribute the work.

44. CA. Art. 54.
45. CA. Art 45.
46. CA. Art. 57.
47. CA. Art. 54(2).

§6. Scope of Exclusive Rights

I. Moral Rights

46. Moral rights are based on the idea to regard the work as a manifestation of author's personality. Accordingly, moral rights are deemed untransferable.

A. Substances of Moral Rights

1. Right of Disclosure

47. The author shall have the right to decide whether or not to make his/her work public.[48] Therefore, making other's work in public without permission constitutes infringement of this moral right. The term 'making it public' means to make the works open to the public by means of performance, broadcasting, exhibitions, or publication.[49] If the author has transferred his/her property right on a work, which is not yet made public, he/she shall be presumed to have given the other party his/her consent to make it public.[50] If the author has transferred by assignment the original of his/her work of art, architectural work or photographic work, which has not been made public, he/she shall be presumed to have given the other party his/her consent to make it public in the manner of exhibition.[51] If a derivative work or compilation work has been made public with the consent of the author, its original shall be also considered to have been made public.[52]

2. Right of Attribution

48. The author shall have the right to indicate his/her name on the original or copy of work, or on the medium of publication by which the work is made public.[53] The person using work shall indicate the author's name in accordance with the author's manner of indication. It is interpreted that author's right to attribute includes the right to hide name. With regard to attribution right issue, Seoul High Court remarks, 'If a web music provider omitted the name of song writer on his web page while indicating the name of singer and producing company, the provider infringed the author's moral right to attribute.'[54]

48. CA. Art. 11.
49. CA. Art. 2. 25.
50. CA. Art. 11(2).
51. CA. Art. 11(3).
52. CA. Art. 11(4).
53. CA. Art. 12.
54. Seoul High Court 2008. 9. 23 – 2007 Na 70720.

3. Right of Integrity

49. The author shall have a right to maintain the integrity of the content, form, and title of his/her work.[55] If the modification of the work is minor enough not to harm substantial identity of the original work, e.g., simple correction of mistyping, it is not infringement of this right. Given the modification is major enough making it deemed an independent work, it does not infringe the right of integrity at all. Thus, the infringement of this right subsists somewhere between these two extremes:

> If a mobile company cut out some parts or abbreviated copyrighted music without consent for ring back tone or bell sound service, it constitutes author's moral right to preserve integrity.[56]

B. Relevant Norms

1. Inalienability

50. Author's moral rights shall belong exclusively to the author. Thus, the author cannot transfer his/her moral right to others.[57]

2. Prohibition of Defaming Use of a Work

51. An act of utilizing a work in a manner prejudicial to the honour or reputation of the author shall be considered to be an infringement of his/her moral rights.[58] It is regarded as a new moral right established through the Copyright Act Amendment of 2011. This provision draws a line between fair use and infringement in moral right's aspect. Thus, defaming use of work beyond author's sound tolerance constitutes infringement; however, such standard of tolerance is decided not by author's subjective view but by judge eyes.

3. Revision, Addition, or Reduction of Work

52. When the exclusive publication right holder republishes the work, the author may revise, add, or reduce the contents of the work to the extent that it is justified.[59] This is a rule to protect author's moral interest for the development or renewal of original work.

55. CA. Art. 13.
56. Seoul High Court 2008. 9. 23 – 2007 Na 70720.
57. CA. Art. 14.
58. CA. Art. 124(2).
59. CA. Art. 58-2. (1).

II. Property Rights

53. Property right of copyright comprises right of reproduction, public performance, public transmission, exhibition, distribution, rental, and making derivative work. Right of public transmission has subcategories of internet transmission right, broadcasting right, and digital audio transmission right. Each property right of copyright may be assigned or licensed separately. Property right functions in a manner to prohibit other from unpermitted use, enabling right holder to recoup his/her investment toward the work.

A. *Right of Reproduction*

1. Definition

54. The author shall have the right to reproduce his/her work.[60] The term 'reproduction' means a fixing on a tangible object temporarily or permanently or a remaking by means of printing, photographing, copying, sound or visual recording, or other means. In cases of architectural structures, it means to execute construction works in accordance with the models or plans for the relevant construction works.[61]

Copyright Act stipulates that 'temporary reproduction' is also a type of reproduction providing, 'the term reproduction means a fixing on a tangible object temporarily or permanently'. On the other hand, temporary reproduction entails many types of immunity in the context of infringement. To explain concretely:

– Where temporary reproduction meets fair use standard in general.[62]
– Where temporary reproduction meets fair use standard of private reproduction.[63]
– Where an user reproduces copyrighted work to the extent deemed necessary for smooth and efficient information processing in computer.[64]
– Where a legitimate possessor of copyrighted program reproduces it to hedge against destruction, damage, or deterioration of the program.[65]
– Where online service provider's immunity rule for reproduction is applied.[66]

2. Decision of Plagiarism

55. Plagiarism constitutes infringement of reproduction right. To be a plagiarism, substantial similarity between two works and junior worker's accessibility to senior work must be attested. To decide substantial similarity, two methods are used: comparing total and intuitive images of the works and comparing 'expressions' left

60. CA. Art. 16.
61. CA. Art. 2. 22.
62. CA. Art. 35-3.
63. CA. Art. 30 or Art. 101-3. 4.
64. CA. Art. 35-2.
65. CA. Art. 101-5.
66. CA. Art. 102.

after filtering out the 'ideas' from mass of the works. Said methods may be used respectively or bilaterally.

In addition to substantial similarity, the junior worker should have relied on the senior work to be a plagiarism. This reliance may be presumed by circumstantial facts such as junior worker's accessibility toward senior work and striking similarity between two works. If junior worker succeeds to attest direct or indirect grounds that his/her work was made independently and the similarity between two works are a result of coincidence, this presumption shall be overturned.

Copyright protection is rendered only to the original creativity. Thus, in deciding similarity between two works, one should strip off part of ideas and expressions taken from public domain and only the remaining parts shall be subject to comparison.[67]

B. *Right of Public Performance*

56. The author shall have the right to perform his/her work publicly.[68] Public performance means opening to public the works, stage performances, music records, or broadcasting by staging, playing, singing, orally narrating, reciting, screening, reproducing, or other methods.[69] Public performance is distinguished from broadcasting in that the contents are transferred directly to human senses, whereas the broadcasting means transmission of contents from device to device by means of wire or wireless.

C. *Right of Public Transmission*

57. The author shall have the right to transmit his/her work in public.[70] Public transmission means transmitting works, stage performances, music records, broadcasting, or database by means of radio communication or wire communication so that the public may receive them or make access to them.[71] Public transmission has subcategories of broadcasting, internet transmission, and digital audio transmission.

1. Broadcasting Right

58. 'Broadcasting' means transmitting sound, image, or sound and image so that the public may receive it simultaneously.[72] The reception here is defined as reception by machinery devices.

67. SCt. 2010. 11. 11 – 2009 Da 16742.
68. CA. Art. 17.
69. CA. Art. 2. 3.
70. CA. Art. 18.
71. CA. Art. 2. 7.
72. CA. Art. 2. 8.

2. Internet Transmission Right

59. 'Internet Transmission' means providing works of digital contents so that public may make access at any time and place of their choice.[73] Internet transmission is distinguished from broadcasting in that the public may individually select time to take contents, whereas the public are simultaneously exposed to the contents in broadcasting. With regard to linking services on internet, Supreme Court adjudicates it neither a reproduction nor an internet transmission of work as it merely lets the web surfer transfer from one site to another.[74]

3. Digital Audio Transmission Right

60. 'Digital Audio Transmission' means the transmission of sound in digital way at the request of the public to have them receive contents simultaneously.[75] From its nature, digital audio transmission is a kind of broadcasting, which Copyright Act sorts out as a separate category. After all, transmission of contents on the internet may be categorized as either type of the followings:

- Transmission of 'image', 'sound', or 'sound and image', which the public receive simultaneously: broadcasting.
- Transmission of 'sound' in digital way, which the public receive simultaneously: digital audio transmission.
- Transmission of 'image', 'sound', or 'sound and image', which the public may access at individual timing: internet transmission.

D. Exhibition Right

61. The author shall have the right to exhibit the original or reproduction of his/her work of art, etc.[76] The objects of exhibition are defined as work of art, architectural work and photographic work.[77] Copyright Act has a provision to alleviate the tension between copyright holder's exhibition right and copyrighted material owner's property right. Article 35(1) stipulates:

- The copyrighted material's owner may exhibit the work in its original form.
- If the work is to be permanently exhibited on the street, in the park, on the outside of the wall of a building, or other place open to the public, the same shall not apply.

73. CA. Art. 2. 10.
74. SCt. 2010. 3. 11 – 2009 Da 4343.
75. CA. Art. 2. 11.
76. CA. Art. 19.
77. CA. Art. 19; Art. 11(3).

E. Distribution Right

1. In General

62. 'Distribution' means a transfer or rental of the original or its reproduction of the work to the public with or without payment.[78] The author shall have the right to distribute the original or reproduction of his/her work: provided, that the original or reproduction of the work has been offered to a deal by means of sales with permission of the relevant holder of author's property right, the same shall not apply.[79] The object of distribution is restricted to material things, entailing transmission of material occupation. Thus, disseminating digital file on internet is not distribution, while it conforms to public transmission on the internet.

2. Exhaustion

63. Once the copyrighted material or its copy has been sold legitimately under right holder's consent, the copyright holder's right of distribution exhausts, attributing it to the property right holder of copyrighted material or its copy. Exhaustion happens only to distribution right and the other copyrights such as right of reproduction, public performance, public transmission etc., are not affected by sales of copyrighted material and remains to copyright holder. This is because the object of transfer is material itself, not rights. In addition, digital file transmission cannot cause exhaustion as material occupation and transfer of digital file is unimaginable.

3. Exhaustion and Parallel Import

64. No Supreme Court case has promulgated whether parallel import is legitimate or not in copyright law's context so far. Commentators tend to refer that parallel import is lawful under the perception of international exhaustion of copyright. Such standpoint is affiliated with free trade and consumers interests in international commerce of copyrighted materials. Article 124(1)-1 is a ground of such idea:

> To import the objects made by an act which would be an infringement of copyright if they were made within Korea at the time of such importation, shall be considered to be infringement of copyright.

Reverse interpretation of this provision leads to the conclusion that parallel importation is legitimate as the imported materials are 'not' the objects made by an act which would be an infringement if they were made within Korea; they are 'genuine' goods supplied by the copyright holder.

78. CA. Art. 2. 23.
79. CA. Art. 20.

F. Rental Right

65. The author shall have the right to rent the commercial music records or computer programs for the purpose of profit making.[80] This rule constitutes an exception of exhaustion rule. As aforementioned, it is principle that the copyright holder who transferred his/her copyrighted material may not control following transfer or exploitation of work due to exhaustion rule. However, the law allows copyright holder to reach through rental business after sales of copyrighted materials, because such business may affect right holders interest in the market, seriously undermining the chances of further sales of copyrighted materials. The subjects of rental right are defined to phonorecord and computer program for sales. Hence, other materials such as books or DVD are not subjects to rental right.

G. Right of Making Derivative Works

66. The author shall have the right to produce and utilize a derivative work based on his/her original work.[81] 'Derivative work' means a creative work produced by means of translation, arrangement, alteration, dramatization, or cinematization, etc., of an original work.[82] To be derivative work, the junior work must be a new work and demonstrate incremental creativity to senior work. At the same time, it must maintain certain degree of similarity with it, not totally departing from senior work. If the junior work stays at the simple similarity of original work, it is reproduction, whereas the junior work demonstrating totally different merit with original work is a new and independent work. In other words, derivative work means a work subordinate to but differentiated from original work.

The additional proportion of creativity in derived work belongs to the junior worker regardless that he/she got permission from the original author or not for producing derivative work. Making derivative work without consent is copyright infringement of the original work but it does not prevent the subsistence of deriver's authorship for the final work. The deriver's right subsists only for the creativity portion he added. Hence, the third party that uses the derived work has to remunerate both authors for each proportion of their creativity in the final work.

§7. Limitations or Exemptions to the Scope of Copyright Protection

67. The moral rights and property rights of copyright are to be limited in certain conditions. Copyright Act provides general fair use rule along with number of individual fair use rules. In addition, copyright license is deemed to exist under certain conditions and copyright exercise is limited where it is regarded as 'abuse of right'.

80. CA. Art. 21.
81. CA. Art. 22.
82. CA. Art. 5.

I. Limitations of Moral Rights

A. *Limitations of Attribution Rights*

68. The obligation of attribution shall not apply where deemed unavoidable in the light of the nature of a work as well as the purpose and manner of its utilization.[83] Accordingly, the user may omit the author's name or indicate it in different way if it meets circumstances of exemption provided.

B. *Limitation of Integrity Right*

69. No author shall raise an objection to a modification falling under any of the following:[84]

(1) In cases of using a work for educational purpose and deemed unavoidable for the purpose of school education.
(2) Extension, rebuilding, or other modifications of an architectural structure.
(3) Modification of computer program within the limit of due compatibility.
(4) Modifications within the limit as deemed unavoidable in the light of the nature of a work as well as the purpose and manner of its utilization (this rule does not apply when modification of substantial contents of work entails).

II. Limitations of Property Rights

A. *Reproduction for Judicial Proceedings, Etc.*

70. It shall be permissible to reproduce a work if and to the extent deemed necessary for the purpose of judicial proceedings and of internal use in the legislative or administrative organs: provided, that the same shall not apply where such reproduction unreasonably prejudices the interests of the holder of author's property right in the light of the kinds of work as well as the number of copies and the forms of reproduction.[85]

B. *Use of Political Speech, Etc.*

71. Political speeches delivered in public and statements made in public, in the court, the National Assembly or local councils may be utilized in some way or other:

83. CA. Art. 12(2).
84. CA. Art. 13(2).
85. CA. Art. 23.

provided, that the speeches and statements of the same author are utilized after compilation, the same shall not apply.[86]

C. Use for Purpose of School Education

72. Copyright can be limited for purpose of school education under certain conditions. Pertinent cases and types of admissible use are consolidated in following table:

Provisions	*User*	*Substance of Use*	*Pay for Use*[87]
Article 25(1)	Institutions of elementary school, middle school or high school, etc.	A work already made public may be reproduced in textbooks.	Shall pay appropriate remuneration for relevant copyright holders.
Article 25(2)	Institutions of kindergarten, elementary school, middle school, high school, or university, etc.	For educational purpose, one may reproduce, distribute, perform in public, exhibit, and transmit in public the part of the works[88] already made in public.	Shall pay appropriate remuneration for relevant copyright holders, except for the use under the level of high school.
Article 25(3)	Students of kindergarten, elementary school, middle school, high school, or university, etc.	May reproduce; transmit on the internet for educational purpose.	

D. Use for Current News Reporting

73. In cases of reporting current events by means of broadcasting, newspapers or by other means, it shall be permissible to reproduce, distribute, perform publicly, and transmit publicly a work seen or heard in the relevant courses, to the extent

86. CA. Art. 24.
87. CA. Art. 25(4).
88. Exceptionally, when it is inevitable to use whole work in light of the character, purpose, form of the work, one may utilize whole work.

justified by the reporting purpose.[89] This is because it will seriously harm the effectiveness of news reporting to enforce permission for the works unavoidably get involved on the way of reporting, and most copyright infringement in such situation is minor and unintended.

E. Reproduction, Etc., of Current News Articles or Editorials

74. Current new articles or editorials inserted in the newspapers and internet newspapers may be reproduced, distributed, or broadcasted by other media organizations: provided, that there is an indication prohibiting the use thereof, the same shall not apply.[90] In contrast with pure and fractional description of news facts, these types of reports fall within the scope of copyright in principle. However, the need of free reproduction and dissemination is also high for people's right of access toward news and function of media. In practice, however, the capability of copyright holder's prohibition seriously deters the application of this exemption.

F. Quotation from Works Made Public

1. Conditions of Fair Quotation

75. Works already made public may be quoted for news report, criticism, education, research, etc., in compliance with the fair practices within the reasonable extent.[91] The conditions of fair quotation are:

(1) Use of published work.
(2) For the purpose of report, criticism, education, and research, etc.: Not only non-commercial purpose meets this standard but use in commercial purpose also does. However, the commercial purpose generally narrows the possibility of fairness.
(3) Reasonable scope of use: In light of quantity and quality of use, the quoting part must take main portion, while the quoted part is subordinate to be a support, ground, reference, or ornament of quoting work.[92]
(4) To comply with the fair practices within the reasonable extent: With regard to this condition, the pertinent indication of source becomes critical standard of fairness.

2. Internet Search Service and Court's Lenient Interpretation of *Quotation*

76. Supreme Court interprets the scope of 'quotation' broadly in internet search service. It remarks that aggregation and display of works as search results in portal

89. CA. Art. 26.
90. CA. Art. 27.
91. CA. Art. 28.
92. SCt. 1990. 10. 23 – 90 Daka 8845.

site is occasionally regarded as 'quotation' despite the fact that there is no main work to which quoted part subordinates. A pertinent case was about a liability of an internet search service provider.[93] In this case, a company of internet portal service collected relevant images requested by users and minimized them into thumbnail images before providing. In ruling, Supreme Court considered that: (1) the works were already made public by the photographer on his website, (2) defendant's main purpose of providing thumbnail images was to meet user's need of information than exhibition or sales of images, (3) it was not substantial use of original work in that the size of used image was too small and the resolution becomes too low once enlarged, (4) the thumbnail images hardly substituted original work in the market as photographer's internet address was shown below, linking the purchasers of photo to original author's web-site; (5) the users also regard thumbnail images as indexes to link to original site; and (6) the public function of internet search services to provide information would be heavily frustrated if adjudicated otherwise. Upon consideration of these, court adjudicated defendant's act to display plaintiff's photos in thumbnail images on its search-result page as fair quotation of copyrighted works. Meanwhile, there is another case of lower court, which decided displaying thumbnail images of big size and high resolution as infringement, as such thumbnail images could substitute the purchase of original photos.[94]

G. *Public Performance and Broadcasting for Non-profit Purposes*

1. Public Performance and Broadcasting of Works Already Made Public[95]

77. Works already made public can be performed publicly and broadcasted free under the conditions that it is done, for non-profit purposes, without charging any fee from audience, and without paying any guarantee to the stage performers.

2. Public Performance of Commercial Music Records or Cinematographic Works

78. It is permissible to perform publicly any commercial music records or cinematographic works, if no benefit in return for the relevant public performance is received from audience or spectators.[96] The examples of public performance of no benefit in return are playing CD in the restaurant or coffee shop for the clients, playing movie DVD in express bus, bus terminal room for the travellers, etc. Indirect commercial purpose is permissible as long as payment is not collected for performance. Supreme Court interprets the term 'commercial music record' here narrowly as otherwise interpretation may harm the copyright holder's interest seriously. Consequently, the CDs specially ordered and made to be played in a franchise coffee

93. SCt. 2006. 2. 9 – 2005 Do 7793.
94. Seoul High Court, 2006. 12. 26. – 2006 Na 24157.
95. CA. Art. 29(1).
96. CA. Art. 29(2).

shop are not in this immunity as they are not music records *sold to public commercially*.[97] On the other hand, a lower court recently promulgated[98] that the music supplied by streaming service and played in department store is equitable with music played by commercially sold records.[99]

The limitation of this rule is applied only for direct performance. Thus, if one performs contents of commercial music records or cinematographic works in public through broadcasting other than performing it directly to public, he is not privileged with this immunity. Further, Copyright Act stipulates various exceptional places where this immunity rule is inoperable: department stores, shopping centres, hotels, golf courses, ski slopes, airplanes, trains, ships, etc. This is because it will seriously undermine right holders interest if the immunity rule is applied leniently to those public places where mass of copyrighted contents are consumed in general.

H. Reproduction for Private Use

79. Copyright Act has provided reproduction for private use as a type of representative fair use. Taking account that reproduction is most ordinary type of use for copyrighted works, this provision has functioned as a general rule of fair use in Copyright Act. This article survived through the Copyright Act amendment in 2012 to adopt 'general rule of fair use', keep on playing the role in parallel to protect users from infringement allegation.

1. Statute

80. It shall be permissible for a user to reproduce in private, without any commercial purposes, a work already made public, within the limit of personal, family, or the equivalent use.[100] The purpose simply to cut cost of purchase is not deemed commercial. Whereas, majority of commentators and courts regard the reproduction conducted internally in company as commercial.

2. Indirect Infringement of Reproduction Right

a. The Relation Between Direct and Indirect Infringement

81. General rule of torts in Korea demands direct infringement as prerequisite of indirect infringement, i.e., abetting or aiding of direct infringement. Meanwhile, as large portion of personal reproductions (direct infringement) are private use (fair use) in internet circumstances, there is no room for indirect infringement to exist if one interprets said rule of tort strictly. In the same logic, the party, which provides

97. SCt. 2012. 5. 10 – 2010 Da 87474.
98. Seoul High Court 2013. 11. 28 – 2013 Na 2007545.
99. As explained below, playing commercially sold record in department store is out of immunity, and the department store shall pay royalty to copyright holders, however.
100. CA. Art. 30.

the method (program), which enables illegal digital file sharing could evade indirect infringement allegation as long as it is utilized for private reproductions. This may encourage widespread share of illegal digital files causing serious harms to copyright holders. Downloading infringing files through P2P program or web-hard service is generally non-commercial reproduction for personal, family, or the equivalent use, constituting no direct infringement at all. If individual downloading of illegal file is uncontrolled as such, the programs or convenience supply to enable massive downloading by numberless parties are out of legal control either. To cope with this situation and impose indirect infringement liability to them, courts have toned down the strictness of direct infringement in those situations, i.e., toned up the strictness for private fair use immunity.

b. *Soribada* Case

82. This case may be titled as a *Korean version of Grokster Case*, in which Supreme Court imposed indirect infringer's liability against P2P program providers of decentralized model named Soribada. Court reasoned:[101]

> File downloading with Soribada program is done massively on internet among anonymous users who do not have any acquaintance but concurrent connection. Unpaid reproductions of copyrighted files through such sharing mechanism are no longer deemed private as a whole, regardless that the reproduction happens privately at individual connector's level. Thus, to provide P2P program which facilitates illegal massive reproductions of digital file is recognized as *aiding* of copyright infringement, attributing indirect infringement liability to provider.

Recently, courts apply this norm to regulate web-storage service through which illegal file sharing of movies, etc., are done. Supreme Court reasoned:[102]

> Private use exemption may not apply for downloading of illegally copied movie files. Otherwise, the copyright infringement for a work would be eternally repeated and maintained on internet. Hence, the downloader who was aware of the illegality of pertinent files is not a fair user despite that it is reproduction under private purpose. Finally, the web-storage provider who is *in dolus eventualis* about this infringement is entitled as indirect infringer who *abetted* or *aided* infringement, providing chances or conveniences to infringers.

83. It is to be noted that Korean Copyright Act does not stipulate, 'downloader of illegally copied file is unqualified as fair user' as German, French, or Japanese copyright law provides. Accordingly, it is practically hard to control individual downloader of illegal files as infringer, while the aiders of such acts are controlled

101. SCt. 2007. 12. 14 – 2005 Do 872.
102. SCt. 2012. 5. 10 – 2011 Do 12131.

as indirect infringer as aforementioned. One might say there is certain legal dissonance where indirect infringer exists without direct infringer. The logical integrity has given its way to policy goal in order to control provider of copyright infringing methods.

3. Reproduction by Copying Apparatus in Public Use

84. The exemption of reproduction for private use shall not apply to the case of reproductions by copying apparatus installed for the use by the general public.[103] This prevents the copying apparatus providers from abusing fair use rule as a method of making money; they have public to reproduce copyrighted work under fair use immunity and take advantage by charging fee for use of copying devices.

4. Special Rules for Computer Program

85. Copyright Act separately provides limitations of property right for computer program in Article 101-3, and 101-3. 4, stipulating, 'One may reproduce copyrighted computer program, provided, it is under purpose of private use in restricted area such as home.'

I. Temporary Sound or Video Recordings by Broadcasting Service Providers

86. Broadcasting service providers may make temporary sound or video recordings of a work for the purpose of their own broadcasting and by means of their own facilities. Such works may not be kept for a period exceeding one year from the date of sound or visual recording.[104] Exceptionally, it may be kept more than one year if kept at secured places prescribed by Presidential Decree.

J. Exhibition or Reproduction of Works of Art, Etc.

87. Copyright Act promotes harmonization of interests among the author, the owner of copyrighted material, and the public to enjoy the contents of copyrighted work. To achieve this goal, Article 35 provides:

(1) The owner of the artistic works, architectural works, and photographic works may exhibit the work in its original form and the copyright owner cannot claim exhibition right against it.
(2) If they are permanently exhibited on the street, in the park, on the outside of the wall of a building, or other place open to the public, the owner has to get permission from copyright owner.

103. CA. Art. 30. Proviso.
104. CA. Art. 34.

(3) Public may reproduce and use the artistic works, architectural works, and photographic works exhibited in public places, so long as the use is not unreasonably excessive. On the other hand, this rule does not apply in any of the following cases:
- where a building is reproduced into another building;
- where a sculpture or painting is reproduced into another sculpture or painting;
- where the reproduction is made in order to exhibit permanently at an open place;
- where the reproduction is made for the purpose of selling its copies.

K. Temporary Reproduction in Course of Using Works, Etc.

88. Where a person uses works on a computer, he/she may temporarily reproduce such works in that computer to the extent deemed necessary for the purpose of smooth and efficient information processing. However, if the main use of work constitutes infringement, such temporary reproduction also is infringement of reproduction right.[105]

L. Fair Use of Copyrighted Work

89. As long as use of others copyrighted work neither unduly harm an author's legitimate profits nor conflict with normal method of utilizing works, a person may use work for the purpose of coverage, criticism, education, research, etc.[106] This is a *catch-all* fair use rule against property right. As described above, Copyright Act enumerates number of respective fair use rules for copyrighted work. This clause is a sequel of KOR-US FTA presented to reinforce such individual provisions. Due to its short legislative history, it is not easy to find court cases, which applied this general rule of fair use so far. Article 35-3 stipulates four factors to be considered in determining fair use:

- Purposes and characters of use, such as for-profit or non-profit.
- Types and uses of works.
- Proportions of used parts in the entire works and their importance.
- Influence of the using works over potential market value of used works.

III. Compulsory License of Copyrighted Work

90. Copyright Act provides several compulsory license rules as the followings. This is to invigorate reasonable exploitation of copyrighted works under specific circumstances where license negotiation is impossible or failed.

105. CA. Art. 35-2.
106. CA. Art. 35-3.

A. Exploitation of Works Whose Holder of Author's Property Right Is Unknown

91. When a person trying to get a license for a work failed to locate copyright holder in spite of due diligence of search, he/she can use the work by depositing a compensation money as determined by the Minister of Culture, Sports and Tourism.[107] This rule is to allow reasonable exploitation of 'orphan works' on behalf of public's interest.

B. Broadcasting of Works Made Public

92. Where a broadcasting organization, which intends to broadcast a work already made public for the sake of the public benefit, has negotiated with the holder of author's property rights but failed to reach an agreement, it may broadcast the work with approval of the Minister of Culture, Sports and Tourism and by paying or depositing a compensation money as determined by the Minister of Culture, Sports and Tourism.[108]

C. Production of Commercial Music Records

93. If a commercial music record has been sold for the first time in Korea and after the expiry of three years from the date of the first sale, and if a person who intends to produce a commercial music record has failed to reach an license agreement, he/she may produce the music record by paying or depositing a compensation money under the standards and process determined by the Minister of Culture, Sports and Tourism.[109] This is to prevent the recording company from monopolizing recording right excessively through exclusive contract with musical authors, and to invigorate musical reproduction, along with market function.

§8. DURATION OF PROTECTION

I. Duration Period

94. The moral rights of an author expire with the death of the author, while it can be enforced after his/her death against the 'defaming use' of the work.[110] The author's property rights to a work shall exist during the lifetime of an author and seventy years after author's death.[111] The property right of copyright to an employee's work and cinematographic work shall exist for a period of seventy years as

107. CA. Art. 50.
108. CA. Art. 51.
109. CA. Art. 52.
110. CA. Art. 14(2).
111. CA. Art. 39(1).

from when it has been made public.[112] The neighbouring right of performer begins to exist when there is a performance, and continues for seventy years as from the first date of next year.[113] The neighbouring right of sound recording producer begins to exist when the sound is recorded, and continues for seventy years as from the first date of next year.[114] The neighbouring right of broadcasting service provider begins to exist when the contents are broadcasted, and continues for fifty years as from the first date of next year.[115]

II. Registration

A. *Registration Office; Registrable Rights*

95. Ministry of Culture, Sports and Tourism is responsible for the registration affairs and, the task is committed to Korean Copyright Commission by the law. Registration is subject to Copyrights,[116] Neighboring Rights, and Database rights.

B. *Subjects to Register*

1. Facts Relevant with Works[117]

96. Following facts about works are to be registered:

- Personal data of author: name, nationality, and address.
- Data of works: title, category, date of creation, and information relevant to publication.
- For derivative works, information about original works.
- For joint works, the share of ownership.

2. Facts Relevant with Rights[118]

97. Following issues about right are to be registered:

- Assignment; restriction of disposal; establishment of exclusive publication right.[119]
- Establishment; transfer; alteration; extinguishment; restriction of disposal for pledge of right.

112. CA. Art. 41; Art. 42.
113. CA. Art. 86(1), (2).
114. Ibid.
115. Ibid.
116. Including Computer Program Copyright.
117. CA. Art. 53(1); CA. Presidential Decree Art. 24.
118. CA. Art. 54.
119. Including, transfer; alteration; extinguishment; restriction of disposal for exclusive publication right.

C. *Submission of Copy*

98. To application documents, drawings, photos, or media of electronic recording shall be attached so that the contents of the work can be perceived. For a computer program to be registered, a copy loaded on electronic media shall be submitted.[120]

D. *Reviewing Authority of Registration Office*

99. It is often questioned to what extent Korean Copyright Commission is to review the applied works. Supreme Court adjudicated that the Commission has authority to review the formality of application documents only. Consequently, the Commission has no authority to decide creativity, scope, or belonging of right; whereas it may refuse registration in the case that applied work is apparently out of subject matter categories. The practice of Commission also follows such guidelines.

E. *Effects of Registration*

100. The person who is registered as the author shall be presumed to be the author of the registered work, and the work whose date of creation or initial publication is registered shall be presumed as such.[121] The registered copyright shall be effective against the third party from the time registration has been affected.[122]

§9. Neighbouring Rights

101. Copyright law renders some property rights and moral rights to the parties who contribute to the expression and dissemination of works. The scopes of these neighbouring rights vary along with the categories of right holders.

I. Holders of Neighbouring Rights

A. *Performers*

102. 'Performer' means a person who gives a stage performance by expressing works through acting, dancing, playing, singing, orally narrating, reciting, or other artistic methods or by expressing things other than works in a similar way, including a person who conducts, directs, or supervises a stage performance.[123]

---

120. CA. Enforcement Rule Art. 6(2) 1; Art. 6(3).
121. CA. Art. 53(3).
122. CA. Art. 54.
123. CA. Art. 2-4.

B. *Sound Recording Producer*

103. 'Sound recording producer' means a person who makes an overall plan and takes charge of fixing sound into records, which excludes the audiovisual work.[124]

C. *Broadcasting Service Provider*

104. 'Broadcasting service provider' means a person who engages in broadcasting business.[125]

II. Substance of Neighbouring Rights[126]

A. *Performer's Neighbouring Rights*

1. The Objects of Protection

105. The objects of performer's neighbouring rights are live performance, performance being broadcasted live, performance fixed on a sound record, performance fixed as an audiovisual work.

2. Property Rights

106. Property rights vested to neighbouring right holders are as the following:

(1) For live performance: right of reproduction, internet transmission, broadcasting, public performance.
(2) For performance being broadcasted live: right of, reproduction, internet transmission, broadcasting.
(3) For performance fixed on a sound recording: right of reproduction, internet transmission, distribution, rental:
   - Where a performer consented fixation, merely remuneration claim is possible for broadcasting of commercial sound recording; public performance of commercial sound recording; digital audio transmission.
   - Where a performer did not consent fixation, the performer can claim right of reproduction, internet transmission, distribution, rental, broadcasting.
(4) For performance fixed as an audiovisual work:
   - Where a performer consented fixation, the doctrine of *presumption of transfer for property right* prevails attributing right of reproduction, distribution, internet transmission, broadcasting to producer.

124. CA. Art. 2-6.
125. CA. Art. 2-9.
126. CA. Art. 64 through 93.

– Where a performer did not consent fixation, he/she enjoys right of reproduction, distribution, internet transmission, broadcasting.

3. Moral Rights

107. Rights of, attribution and preserving integrity are conferred as moral rights.

B. Sound Recording Producer's Neighbouring Rights

1. The Object of Protection

108. The object of protection is sound fixed on a record.

2. Property Rights

109. Sound recording producer is given right of reproduction, distribution, rental, and internet transmission. In addition, remuneration claim is capable for broadcasting of commercial sound recording, public performance of commercial sound recording, and digital audio transmission.

C. Broadcasting Service Provider's Neighbouring Rights

1. The Object of Protection

110. The object of protection is contents broadcasted.

2. Property Rights

111. Rights of reproduction, simultaneous relay broadcasting, and public performance are conferred on broadcasting service provider.[127] Neighbouring rights in Copyright Act may be consolidated as in the following table.

127. Public performance right of broadcasting service provider is exercisable only to the performance at a public place, charging fee to the audiences.

<table>
<tr><th></th><th>Object of Protection</th><th colspan="2">Property Rights</th><th>Remuneration Rights</th><th>Moral Rights</th></tr>
<tr><td rowspan="3">Performer</td><td>– performance live
– performance being broadcasted live</td><td colspan="2">– reproduction
– internet transmission
– broadcasting
– public performance (not for performance broadcasted live)</td><td></td><td rowspan="3">– Attribution
– Integrity</td></tr>
<tr><td rowspan="2">performance fixed in a sound record</td><td colspan="2">– reproduction
– internet transmission
– distribution; rental</td><td></td></tr>
<tr><td>broadcasting,
(i) case of consent for fixation: not given, but remuneration rights
(ii) case of no consent for fixation: given</td><td>No public performance right, as it is given only to public performance live.</td><td>– remuneration for broadcasting of commercial records
– remuneration for digital audio transmission of records
– remuneration for public performance of commercial records</td></tr>
</table>

	Object of Protection	*Property Rights*		*Remuneration Rights*	*Moral Rights*
	performance fixed as an audiovisual work	(i) case of no consent for fixation: reproduction; distribution; internet transmission; broadcasting (ii) case of consent to fixation: doctrine of *presumption of transfer to producer* prevails for rights enumerated in (i).			

	Object of Protection	*Property Rights*	*Remuneration Rights*	*Moral Rights*
Sound Recording Producer	sound fixed on a record	reproduction; distribution; rental; internet transmission	– remuneration for broadcasting of commercial records – remuneration for digital audio transmission of records – remuneration for public performance of commercial records	
Broadcasting Service Provider	contents broadcasted	reproduction; simultaneous relay broadcasting; public performance		

III. Limitations of Neighbouring Rights

112. Limitations for property right of copyright apply to neighbouring rights.[128] One may use copyrighted work without getting permission from neighbouring right holder once the use meets conditions of fair use.

IV. Relation between Copyright and Neighbouring Right

113. Neighbouring rights shall not be understood as affecting copyright.[129] This implies the user of performed, sound recorded or broadcasted contents must get separate permission from copyright holder of those contents as well as the performer, producer of sound recording, or broadcasting service provider. Supreme Court adjudicated:

> Those who make compilation CDs with excerpted songs from original albums and distribute them shall get permission from both producer of original albums and authors of excerpted songs. This is because such deeds constitute infringement of reproduction right and distribution right of original author, along with album producer, i.e., a neighboring right holder.[130]

§10. Infringement and Remedies

I. Types of Infringement

A. *Direct Infringement*

114. Direct infringement shall mean any act to harm moral rights or to reproduce, perform publicly, transmit publicly, display publicly, distribute, rent, derive the copyrighted work without right holder's permission. As for remedies, prohibition order is to be rendered on the ground of plaintiff's claim.[131] Damages are available to infringement from wilfulness or negligence.[132] Infringement may exist to other rights protected in Copyright Act such as neighbouring rights, exclusive publication right, and database right.

B. *Indirect Infringement*

115. Indirect infringement shall mean aiding or abetting direct infringement. Indirect infringement also provokes liability, regardless that it is not stipulated in

128. CA. Art. 87(1).
129. CA. Art. 65.
130. SCt. 2006. 7. 13 – 2004 Da 10756.
131. CA. Art. 123.
132. CA. Art. 125.

Copyright Act. Indirect infringement has been mattered mainly with providers of P2P programs or web-storage service, by which many users commit direct infringement under cover of private fair use immunity.

1. P2P Program Provider (*Soribada* Case)

116. Supreme Court reasoned:

> Aid by negligence as with aid by willful negligence satisfies subjective conditions for indirect infringement. To be an aid by negligence, one need not specifically be aware of the place, time, and infringed works or even who is direct infringer; abstract awareness or negligence to possibility of direct infringement is enough. Defendants were actually or possibly aware that their free distribution of P2P program (*Soribada*) and providing server service may facilitate direct infringement on internet. The users of *Soribada* shared and stored MPEG files that were extracted from copyrighted music CDs, infringing reproduction right and internet transmission right; thus, defendants are liable as indirect infringers for the damages copyright holders suffered.[133]

2. Provider of Web-Hard Server

117. Supreme Court also determined liability of indirect infringement to a web-storage service provider.[134] In this case, defendant provided web-storage being aware that the users may utilize it as a media to share infringing files; actually, innumerable users uploaded and downloaded millions of illegal digital copies of movies and music through that storage service.

3. Portal Site Operator

118. Supreme Court also mentioned possibility of indirect infringer's liability for portal site operator (a sort of online service provider). The conditions of indirect infringer's liability for the operator are: (1) that the illegality of posted work is objectively clear in copyright law's context, (2) that operator is aware of situation by notice of copyright holder or spontaneously, and (3) that the control and handling of posted work is technically and economically possible.[135]

4. Limitations of Responsibility for Online Service Provider[136]

119. This is a kind of special rule regulating liability of intermediaries in internet circumstances. Online service providers play essential role to facilitate share and

133. SCt. 2007. 1. 25 – 2005 Da 11626.
134. SCt. 2012. 5. 10 – 2011 Do 12131.
135. SCt. 2010. 3. 11 – 2009 Da 4343.
136. CA. Art. 102 through 104.

transmission of digital contents on internet. Meanwhile, they can be placed on indirect infringer's position when direct infringement happens through their service; this may frustrate supply of such services. Upon consideration of this situation, Copyright Act provides several limitations to online service provider's liability of indirect infringement, and provides procedures they shall comply with. Copyright Act categorizes online service as conduit, caching, storage, and search. The conditions and procedural obligations for each type of service to evade infringement liability are stipulated.

120. If OSP has claimed that copyright infringement is ongoing by means of its service, OSP shall temporarily stop transmitting alleged contents according to statutory procedure; notice such facts to alleged infringer and follow subsequent conditions to resume transmission service. Abiding by this procedural obligation, OSP is free from any allegation of copyright infringement.[137] Where it is technologically impossible for OSP to take measures, OSP shall not be responsible for the infringement.[138] OSP shall not be responsible for monitoring any infringement within its services or actively investigating such infringement.[139]

C. Act Deemed Infringement

1. Importation to Distribute

121. The importation, for the purpose of distribution of objects, which would be infringing if they were made within Korea at the time of such importation, is deemed infringement.[140] The targets of this regulation are imported materials, which would infringe. It is necessary to prevent importation of such materials as they are destined to infringe copyright in the long run. By virtue of this provision, the 'pirate copies of copyrighted work' can be banned at early stage of importation.

2. Possession of Infringing Articles to Distribute

122. The possession, for the purpose of distribution, of objects produced by an act of infringement of copyright by a person who is aware of such facts is deemed infringement.[141] By virtue of this provision, the flow of pirated copy can be banned in advance.

137. CA. Art. 103.
138. CA. Art. 102(2).
139. CA. Art. 102(3).
140. CA. Art. 124(1) 1.
141. CA. Art. 124(1) 2.

3. Business Use of Illegal Copy of Computer Program

123. Business use of illegal copy of computer program by a person who has acquired it knowing such illegality is deemed infringement.[142] This provision prevents use of pirated software and practically pre-empts fair use defence of 'private reproduction' for software. This pre-emption is possible because most of 'business use' is under 'non-private' purpose, and temporary copy of works may well infringe reproduction right in current copyright paradigm.

II. Protection of Technical Measures and Rights Management Information

A. *Protection of Technical Protection Measures*

124. The term 'technical protection measures' means measures to prevent or control the 'access' or 'infringement' to the works:[143]

(1) Principally, no person shall incapacitate technical protection measures by removing, altering, or circumventing such measures.[144]
(2) Principally, no person shall manufacture, import, distribute, transmit, sell or lend, solicit to buy, advertise to sell or lend, store, or possess for distribution the devices to incapacitate technical protection measures. Principally, no person shall provide the service to incapacitate technical protection measures.[145]

B. *Protection of Rights Management Information*

125. The term 'rights management information' refers to any information to indicate the work, right holder, or conditions for use, being attached onto copyrighted material or accompanied with the public performance, execution, or public transmission of the work:[146]

(1) No person shall deliberately remove, alter, or falsely add rights management information.[147]
(2) No person shall distribute rights management information or import it to distribute knowing such information has been removed or altered without authority.[148]

142. CA. Art. 124(1) 3.
143. CA. Art. 2. 28.
144. CA. Art. 104-2(1).
145. CA. Art. 104-2(2).
146. CA. Art. 2. 29.
147. CA. Art. 104-3(1) 1.
148. CA. Art. 104-3(1) 2.

(3) No person shall distribute, perform publicly, publicly transmit, or import to distribute the works, knowing such information has been removed, altered, or falsely added without authority.[149]

III. Remedies

A. *Prohibition Order (Injunction)*

126. As aforementioned, the liability from direct infringement may be held even without wilfulness or negligence. Prohibition order is the most influential and instant remedy against infringement. Article 123 provides:

(1) Copyright holder may demand infringer to suspend such act; may demand a person likely to infringe to take preventive measures.
(2) Copyright holder may also demand infringer to abandon the objects made by infringement.
(3) In the cases of (1), (2), or in the case where a criminal indictment has been filed for infringement, on request of a plaintiff or accuser, the court may issue an order to temporarily suspend the act of infringement, or seize the objects made by the act of infringement, or to take other necessary measures.

B. *Damages*

127. Infringement of copyright and other rights protected in Copyright Act: neighbouring rights, exclusive publication right, and database right (hereinafter, mentioned as only 'copyright'), is an act of 'tort'. Damages are available to torts of wilfulness or negligence in accordance with relevant provisions in Civil Act.[150] However, in most cases, it is hard for plaintiff to prove causal relation between infringement and 'actual damages'. To alleviate this problem and protect plaintiff effectively, Copyright Act provides several special articles of damage calibration rules, which are based upon some legal presumptions.

1. Presumption of Infringer's Profit to Damages

128. If the infringing person has gained any profit by infringement, the relevant amount of profit shall be presumed to be the amount of damages sustained by copyright holder.[151]

149. CA. Art. 104-3(1) 3.
150. Civil Act, Art. 750.
151. CA. Art. 125(1).

2. Reasonable Royalty

129. The copyright holder may choose the amount of reasonable royalty as damages against unpermitted use of copyrighted work.[152] The 'reasonable royalty' here denotes objective amount of money which would have been paid if infringer had gone into a license contract with right holder. If any case of prior license exists, the actual amount of royalty may be standard; if no such case exists, the practical royalty in the field of work shall be criteria deciding reasonable royalty.[153]

3. Presumption of Negligence for Infringement of Registered Works

130. Any person infringed registered work shall be presumed to have committed such infringement out of negligence.[154] In contrast with patent, trademark, and design, registration is not the condition for existence of copyright. Thus, copyright infringer's liability may be denied in light of damages where the subjective condition of wilfulness or negligence is absent, whereas such absence does not affect prohibition order.

4. Statutory Damages

131. Copyright holder may claim considerable damages maximum South Korean Won (KRW) 10 million (maximum KRW 50 million in cases of wilful infringement for commercial purpose) per each work.[155] The work must be registered before infringement to claim statutory damages.[156] Court may use discretion deciding amount of damages within stipulated scopes.[157]

5. Decision of Damages by Discretion

132. Where it is difficult to decide damages by Article 125, court may fix considerable damages on its discretion in the light of total purport and evidence in litigation.[158] This is supplemental rule provided for plaintiff who evidently suffered damages by infringement but eventually failed to prove any of its amounts.

152. CA. Art. 125(2).
153. SCt. 2010. 3. 11 – 2007 Da 76733.
154. CA. Art. 125(4).
155. CA. Art. 125-2(1).
156. CA. Art. 125-2(3).
157. CA. Art. 125-2(4).
158. CA. Art. 126.

6. Comparative Negligence

133. Where plaintiff takes parts in occurrence or expansion of damages, such negligence of plaintiff must be reflected in deciding amount of damages. It is the same in copyright infringement and calibration of damages. In a case, defendant illegally copied plaintiff's copyrighted digital works posted on plaintiff's web page. To petition of plaintiff, Supreme Court answered that plaintiff was able to prevent or minimize damages by setting access denial program or watermark methods. Such negligence to take due measure to prevent damages are to be considered as plaintiff's demerit.[159]

C. Criminal Sanctions

134. In Korea, copyright infringements are subject to criminal sanctions of imprisonment or fine. Penalties paired with individual types of infringement are provided in Articles 136 through 142.

D. Liability of Tort

135. Recently, courts began to adjudicate that deeds, which are not infringement in light of Copyright Act, may suffice cause of tort action by civil law, giving rise to liability. In a case, a defendant who commercially used a visual character of plaintiff's creation was held of tort's liability. In the case, plaintiff's character was not copyrightable subject matter, rather close to idea than expression; however, Supreme Court reasoned commercially appropriating the fruit of other's 'endeavour' shall trigger general tort liability, justifying monetary remunerations.[160]

§11. Overlapping and Relation to Other Intellectual Property Laws

136. Relevant descriptions in design patent, lay-out design, and limitation of trademark use from other's copyright shall be referred to.

159. Sct. 2010. 3. 11. – 2007 Da 76733.
160. SCt. 2012. 3. 29 – 2010 Da 20044.

Chapter 2. Patents

§1. Sources: Legislation

137. Patent Act of Korea was initially enacted on 13 April 1952 (Act No. 238) and has been amended forty times into current version of 22 March 2013 (Act No. 11654). Particularly important amendments among them are as the followings:

- 31 December 1961 (Act No. 950): First to file system; grace period; prior user's right; fifteen years duration of patent
- 5 April 1963 (Act No. 1293): Definition of invention; priority rights
- 1 January 1974 (Act No. 2505): Exclusion of 'New Use of Known Matter Invention' from patentable subject matter; loss of novelty by foreign document published prior to patent application
- 1 September 1981 (Act No. 3325): Alignment of provisions to harmonize with Paris Convention; laying-open of application after eighteen months; commencement of examination procedure solely for requested applications
- 11 November 1982 (Act No. 3566): Establishment of international patent application rules to join PCT
- 1 July 1 1987 (Act No. 3891): Patentability for chemical substance as such and new use of chemical substance; compulsory license for patents domestically unused over three years; extension of patent duration within five years for medical drugs
- 1 September 1990 (Act No. 4207): Addition of asexually reproducible bulbs and foods to patentable subject matters
- 1 July 1996 (Act No. 5080): Reflections of TRIPs contents: broadened conception for use of invention, compulsory license proclamation, extension of patent duration to twenty years etc.; early disclosure of filed invention upon applicant's request
- 1 March 1998 (Act No. 4892): Establishment of trial board in Korean patent office; Patent Court's sole jurisdiction for the appeal of trial decision
- 4 September 2006 (Act No. 7869): Consolidation of employee's invention rules into Promotion of Invention Act
- 1 July 2007 (Act No. 8197): Rendering leniency to specification writing standards; adoption of provisional application system
- 1 July 2011 (Act No. 10716): Adoption of applicant's duty to report relevant arts with invention
- 15 March 2012 (Act No. 11117): Extension of grace period from six months to twelve months; abolition of patent cancellation rule based upon three years' domestic non-use; extension of patent duration to recover loss from delayed examination; adoption of Order of Secrecy in infringement litigations.

The important patent related treaties Korea joined and the dates they came into force are as the followings (date of joining: date of coming into force):

- Paris Convention for the Protection of Industrial Property (1883: 1980).
- Convention Establishing the World Intellectual Property Organization (1967: 1979).
- Patent Cooperation Treaty (1970: 1984).
- Strasbourg Agreement Concerning the International Patent Classification (1971: 1999).
- Budapest treaty (1977: 1988).

Though said treaties basically works as the sources of law for patent, It is rare that a provision of treaty is directly applied to individual case in Korea as National Assembly has been reflecting most of the substance through serial legislations.

§2. Patentable Subject Matter

I. Inventions

A. *Statutory Definition*

138. Patent is subject to inventions. Patent Act stipulates invention as, 'highly advanced creation of technical ideas utilizing laws of nature'.[161] However, the terms of 'advanced creation' here became hollow as it is too abstract as an element of definition and has been practically substituted by conception of 'inventive step'. Accordingly, the term of 'utilizing laws of nature' is critical threshold to invention. Considering there are unlimited sorts of inventions at present or in the future, it is practical to take negative method to exclude which are 'not' inventions, than positive method to demonstrate what inventions are. As categories of non-invention, the following are generally mentioned:

- The law of nature itself: thermodynamics, universal gravity, relativity, etc.
- Anything apparently against law of nature: e.g., eternal engines.[162]
- Abstract idea as such: mathematical methods, simple presentation of information, rule of economy, social science, games, agreements, schemes, etc.
- Simple discovery of pre-existing matters in the nature.
- Aesthetic creations.

B. *'Admitted' Types of Invention*

139. According to classical definition of invention aforementioned, it is hard to categorize computer program and business method into patentable subject matters. It is because computer program is nothing but a sequential function to order machine execute certain process; business method is basically 'schemes of making money'. Under conventional definition, both are close to 'abstract idea', than utilizations of law of nature. Similar dilemma is also seen in gene technology. Many

161. PA Art 2. 1.
162. SCt. 1998. 9. 4 – 98 Hoo 744.

researches and technological investments are conducted to investigate and unveil the 'functions' of certain segments of DNA, which often becomes starting point to develop pertinent genetic drugs or medical treatments. However, one might say simple identification of genetic function of purported DNA is 'discovery' than 'utilization of law of nature', which is excluded from the realm of invention. Taking practical immensity of influence to industry and economy, and giving incentive for continual progress, patent practice has regarded those works as 'inventions' from long ago.

II. Sorts of Inventions

A. *Statutory Categories*

140. Patent Act categorizes invention into 'product' and 'process'.[163] The category of invention plays significant role when patent claim is written. Any kind of invention can be and ought to be categorized either of product or of process and must be described as such in patent claims. Product denotes any type of manmade things, e.g., machine, apparatus, devices, material, compound, composition of matter, mixture, pharmaceuticals, food, microbes, plants, animals, etc. Process means the order of steps to achieve technical purpose, e.g., methods of manufacturing products, using products, manoeuvring products, repairing products, communication, measurement, etc.

B. *Inventions of Theoretical Significance*

141. It is to be noted that each invention mentioned below are named as such due to its characteristics, while it belongs to either category of 'product' or 'process' originally.

1. New Use of Known Matter

142. New Use Known Matter Invention[164] means finding out unrecognized property of known materials. Theoretically, New Use Invention is close to 'discovery' than utilization of law of nature. However, patent practice has qualified it as an invention to encourage pursuers to probe further utility of pre-existing materials. The notion of New Use Invention is not uniform. It is paragon of New Use Invention to discover unknown property and utility of already known matter, but New Use Invention may also subsist over newly composed matters. The reason why New Use Invention is mainly discussed in chemical field is because many recognized compounds are bound to have unrevealed property or utility from the nature of

163. PA Art. 2. 3.

164. Hereinafter, mentioned as 'New Use Invention'.

chemistry as 'field of experiments'. On the other hand, it is hard to imagine discovering new use for pre-existing machine or apparatus.

2. Selection Inventions

143. Selection Invention means selection of individual elements, sub-sets, or sub-ranges, which have not been explicitly mentioned, within a larger known set or range. Selection invention also matters in chemical fields. Selection invention entails novelty problem as its larger set or range is already known, but patent practice qualifies it as independent invention to encourage particularization seeking for unexpected advantages over prior sub-set patents. Due to this norm to precipitate ongoing scour of prior art, the selection invention must pass three parts novelty thresholds that: (1) the claimed range must be narrower, (2) it must be sufficiently distant from preferred known ranges, and (3) it must not be an arbitrary choice of prior art.

3. Computer Program

144. As aforementioned, the question if computer program, a series of mathematical functions, overcomes the hurdle of 'utilization of law of nature' is resolved by practice. Guideline of examination in KIPO stipulates, 'Where data processing with a computer program is specifically executed using a hardware, a data processing unit (machine) operating in association with the computer program; its operating method; and a computer readable medium carrying the computer program are viewed as statutory inventions.'[165]

4. Biotechnology

a. Animals, Microorganisms

145. Mutated animals having technical merit may be patented as such as well as the method of such mutation, or method to use animal.[166] Microorganism inventions are subject to the method of producing microorganism, e.g., isolation culture, artificial mutation, genetic manipulation, and the method of utilizing microorganism to medicines or foods. Articles 2 through 4 of Presidential Decree mandates patent applicants' deposition of microorganism.[167] Any pertinent party may be distributed of microorganism deposited for research or experiments.

---

165. KIPO, Patent Examination Guidelines (2013), Part III. Chapter 1, 4.1.8.; SCt. 2001. 11. 30 – 97 Hoo 2507.
166. KIPO, Patent Examination Guidelines (Biotechnology), (2012), Ch. 5.
167. This rule is in accordance with Budapest treaty, to which Korea has joined.

b. Plants

146. Refer to the descriptions of Chapter 7 (Plant Variety Protection).

c. Gene-Related Inventions

147. Gene-related inventions include DNA fragments, SNP, antisense, vector, recombinant transformant, hybridoma, proteins, recombinant proteins, monoclonal antibodies, etc.[168] Purified DNA is deemed 'chemical product' which does not exist in nature, being subject matter of patent. In many cases, investigation of certain DNA sequence and its utility becomes the crux of inventions. With human genes, the amino acid or DNA sequence to code interferon, interleukin, the utility and function of which are identified have been subject to patent.[169]

5. Business Method

148. KIPO publicized 'guidelines for the examination of e-commerce inventions' in 2000. Namely, this is guidelines for business method (BM) patent examination. BM patent is categorized as a software patent in Korea and general guidelines of software patent examination is applied *mutatis mutandis*. However, the requisite that software shall be connected to a hardware, other than general purpose computer is substantially slackened off in BM invention; thus, it is not rare that software run in a network of general purpose computer is subject to BM patent.

§3. Conditions of Patentability

I. Substantial Conditions

A. Industrial Applicability

1. In General

149. The purpose of patent system is to encourage, protect, and utilize inventions, thereby promoting the development of technology, and to contribute to the development of industry.[170] Hence, the invention must have 'industrial applicability' to be entitled of patent. The examples of invention without industrial applicability are:

- Inventions of unidentified utility.
- Dangerous invention without proper security measure.
- Inoperable invention (including inventions operable only theoretically).

---

168. KIPO, Patent Examination Guidelines (Biotechnology), (2012), Ch. 1.
169. KIPO, Patent Examination Guidelines (Biotechnology), (2012), Ch. 2.
170. PA Art. 1.

As aforementioned, law of nature, subjects apparently against law of nature, simple discovery, aesthetic creation, mere presentation of information, are not 'inventions' as such. However, KIPO's examination guideline exemplifies them also as 'invention without industrial applicability' to filter them out clearly from patentable subject matters.[171]

2. Medical Skills (Surgery, Therapy, Diagnostic Methods, Etc.)

150. Inventions pertinent to medicine are categorized into: (1) inventions of medical apparatus, (2) inventions of medical substance, and (3) inventions of medical skills (surgery, therapy, diagnostic methods, etc.). Like most other countries in the world, Korea regards (1) and (2) as patentable, while (3) is out of patent eligibility. The reason to grant patent for (1) and (2) is to sustain commercial incentive of development. The reason not to grant patent for (3) is that the lives and health of humans are superior to technological advancement towed by patent.[172]

151. Courts and guidelines conventionally have mentioned 'lack of industrial applicability' as reason to deny patentability of medical skills.[173] A method to treat human body by surgery or therapy and a diagnostic method practised on the human body are not considered as 'industrial skills'. However, the borderline between pure medical skills of doctors and other patentable technology in medical treatment are not always clear. Especially in the field of biotechnology and diagnosis, many believe that imprudent negation of patentability would result immense disadvantage to national wealth; therefore, the concept of industrial applicability is interpreted leniently allowing patents under pertinent conditions in these fields. Certain types of medical skills utilizing biotechnology to diagnose or treat human disease are patentable. Guideline provides:

> A method for treating samples that have been extracted from a human body (e.g., blood, urine, skin, hair, cells or tissue) or discharged from a human body (e.g., urine, excrement, placenta, hair and nail) and a method for gathering data by analyzing such samples are considered to be industrially applicable on the assumption that they are composed of separate steps separable from medical practices.[174]

152. Further, in light of aforesaid situation, the method of diagnosis without 'clinical decision of doctor' or simply collecting data is patentable except that it

171. Guideline, Part III, Ch. 1., 4.1.
172. Article 96(2) of Patent Act provides, 'The effects of the patent right for inventions of a medicine manufactured by mixing two or more medicines, or for inventions of processes for manufacturing medicines by mixing two or more medicines, shall not extend to the acts of manufacturing medicines or to medicines manufactured by such acts in accordance with the Pharmaceutical Affairs Act.' This article also implies said superiority of human health to patent right.
173. SCt. 1991. 3. 12 – 90 Hoo 250; SCt. 2006. 8. 25. – 2005 Hoo 1936; Guideline, Part III, Ch. 1., 5.1.
174. Guideline, Part III, Ch. 1., 5.1.

involves the stage to influence human body directly and non-temporarily. Guideline also admits patentability for method of operating a medical device or measurement method with the medical device, where the medical device is newly invented.[175]

B. Novelty

1. Loss of Novelty

153. The novelty of applied invention is denied if: (1) the identical invention is publicly known by description in publicized materials, public performance, or putting on web pages; (2) prior to filing date; (3) in Korea or any other foreign country. As Korea is in First to File System, whether an art is prior one is determined not by the timing of invention but by application. Namely, once an identical art is publicly known before the filing date, it can defeat the novelty of filed invention even where filed invention was produced earlier than said prior art. 'Known public' purports that the prior art was exposed to capability of public's recognition, and the way it became public does not matter (publication, public use, disclosure on internet, etc.). On the other side, 'known public' denotes the information of prior art is disclosed to public without any restriction. Thus, it is not 'known public' once there exists 'obligation of secrecy' by contract or commercial practice, even though it is exposed to capability of public recognition. Such prior art is deemed known to public when the party breached the obligation and actually disclosed it to public.[176]

154. To be a prior art to defeat novelty, it shall be 'identical' with filed invention. 'Identity' here means substantial identity. Thus, the standard is deemed met if the difference between two inventions lies in mere addition, conversion, or deletion of well-known elements, not affecting the technical effect of the filed invention.[177] Where prior art lies in sub-set or range, the novelty of filed invention in larger- set or range is denied. Decision of identity is to be based upon substances of inventions, other than categories or expressions; thus, the inventions of same substance are identical regardless that they belong to different categories (process, product) or are expressed in different format.[178]

2. Non-prejudicial Disclosures: Inventions Not Considered Publicly Known

155. When the invention is disclosed to public by any of the following reasons, it is not deemed in loss of novelty or inventive step so long as the inventor or his/

175. Guideline, Part III, Ch. 1., 5.1.
176. SCt. 2005. 2. 18 – 2003 Hoo 2218.
177. SCt. 2001. 6. 1 – 98 Hoo 1013; SCt. 2003. 2. 26 – 2001 Hoo 1624; Guideline, Part III, Ch. 2.,4.3.
178. SCt. 2004. 10. 14 – 2003 Hoo 2164.

her legitimate successor files patent application within twelve months as from the date such reason happens:

(1) Where a person with the right to obtain a patent caused disclosure before filing date.[179]
(2) Where, against the intention of a person with the right to obtain a patent, the invention was disclosed before filing date.[180]

156. A person who intends to take aforesaid advantage shall submit a document to Commissioner of the KIPO when filing a patent application; the person claiming (1) shall also submit a document proving the relevant facts, within thirty days of the filing date of the patent application.[181] If the aforesaid substantial and procedural conditions are met, the novelty or inventive step of filed invention is not defeated by such prior disclosure.

To be noted, if the substance of filed invention is independently known to public by any third party before filing date, it undoubtedly becomes a prior art to defeat the novelty or inventive step of filed invention. For example, if A exhibits her invention at a fair on 1 May 2014 and filed for patent on 1 October 2014; B separately devised identical invention and laid it open to public on 1 August 2014, the novelty of A's invention shall be destroyed by prior art of B. The norm of non-prejudicial disclosure is applied not only for deciding novelty but also for deciding nonobviousness. Thus, the applicant may claim this rule where she improved her prior invention within the scope of obviousness[182] and file for a patent for such sequel invention.

C. Enlarged Concept of Novelty

157. Article 29(3) of Patent Act stipulates 'enlarged concept of novelty': the substance described in specification or drawings of prior application may be prior art to defeat novelty of later application once it is disclosed after later application. This is an exception of novelty rule as the prior art was not disclosed at the moment of later application. On the other side, if the claim(s) of later application is substantially identical with the claim(s) of prior application, Article 36 (First to File Rule) shall pre-empt the rule of enlarged concept of novelty. There is no application of enlarged concept of novelty rule if the inventor of prior and later application is identical.[183]

179. PA Art. 30. (1) 1., This provision does not apply where such disclosure is caused by the lay-open of patent application or a patent registration in Korea or any foreign country under a treaty or law.
180. PA Art. 30(1) 2.
181. PA Art. 30(2).
182. If the sequel invention in nonobvious enough to obtain patent, there shall be no reason to visit non-prejudicial disclosure rule and the invention may well be examined conceding prior disclosure as prior art.
183. PA Art. 29(3), proviso.

D. *Inventive Step (Nonobviousness)*

158. Inventive step becomes critical issue in most types of patent disputes. The burden of proof about lack of inventive step is disposed to examiner in prosecution or trial against rejections, while it is disposed to infringer after patent is granted.

1. Method to Determine Inventive Step

159. The method to determine inventive step consists of:

(1) Stage to locate pertinent prior art(s).
(2) Stage to determine state of the art in pertinent field (imagining person skilled in the art).
(3) Stage to decide if it is obvious for person skilled in the art to devise present invention based upon said prior art(s).[184]

a. Prior Art

160. As with novelty, the moment of application is threshold to decide whether an art is prior or not against invention applied for patent. The prior art shall belong to relevant field of art with invention applied for patent, not too far for skilled person in the art to refer to. However, courts recently tend to extend the scope of relevant field where prior arts are cited from.[185] Even incomplete invention shall be prior art to refer to determining inventive step.[186] Namely, the inventive step should be denied if main idea of present invention is taken from incomplete prior art and the incremental output is obvious to a skilled person.

b. Person Skilled in the Art

161. A person skilled in the art refers to a hypothetical person who has:

(1) The general knowledge and ability of comprehension in pertinent art,[187] and
(2) the ability to exercise ordinary creativity in selecting materials, changing designs; to use technical means for analysis, experiment, and manufacture.

c. Deciding if Obvious to Person Skilled in the Art

(i) Elimination of Hindsight

162. Supreme Court stipulates, 'To decide inventive step of present patent, the decision-maker should be in position of person skilled in the art that has no

184. Guideline, Part III, Ch. 3, 5.1.
185. SCt. 2008. 7. 10 – 2006 Hoo 2059.
186. SCt. 1996. 10. 29 – 95 Hoo 1302.
187. Guideline, Part III, Ch. 3, 3.2.

information of filed invention. It is improper to have view of a person who has already read the specification of present invention.'[188] Such a retrospective attitude shall cause 'hindsight' inevitably leading decision-maker to underestimate hardship of present invention.

(ii) Comparison of Features and Technical Effects

163. It is common practice to compare features and effects of present invention and prior art(s) to presume nonobviousness. The logic of this practice is that if the difference between two arts is big, it would not be easy for skilled person to be led to present invention from prior art. Further, the more technical effect present invention has, the more motivation skilled person would have had if the solution was obvious; therefore, the late presentation of the invention strongly infers its nonobviousness. In accordance with this idea, following combinations of standard for nonobviousness can be portrayed:

(1) Big difference in features and much advance in effect: (Highly) Nonobvious.
(2) Big difference in features but little advance in effect: Nonobvious.
(3) Small difference in features but much advance in effect: (Highly) Nonobvious.
(4) Small difference in features and little advance in effect: Obvious.

(iii) Elements Representing Obviousness[189]

164. Guideline describes that the followings are indicators of obviousness of present invention:

(1) Suggestions shown in prior art.
(2) Close similarity of a problem to be solved between present invention and prior art.
(3) Close similarity of a function, work, or operation between present invention and prior art.
(4) Close relation of technical fields between present invention and prior art.

If present invention falls on any of the followings, the inventive step from prior art shall be denied:

(1) Replacement with equivalents.
(2) Workshop modification of a design in applying a specific technology.
(3) Partial removal of technical features.
(4) Simple change and limitation of use of the invention.
(5) General application of known art.

(iv) Advantageous Effects to Be Considered

165. If the effect of claimed invention is advantageous in comparison with an effect of prior art, it is taken into consideration as a fact to affirmatively support its

188. SCt. 2007. 8. 24 – 2006 Hoo 138; SCt. 2010. 7. 22 – 2008 Hoo 3551.
189. Guideline, Part III, Ch. 3, 6.1.1. through 6.2.5.

inventive step.[190] In most of the patent cases, technical effect plays significant role in deciding inventive step of patent. This is quite natural if one reminds original goal of patent system: to encourage invention with new and useful effect, aiming for technological development.

(v) Secondary Considerations

166. Many commentators recommend to consider secondary factors such as commercial success, long-felt need, teaching away of prior art, the attitudes of competitors, etc., as 'objective indicia' in deciding nonobviousness. However, courts accept this idea very passively so far. Dozens of court decisions have mentioned 'commercial success' as supplementary factor of obviousness decision either positively or negatively.[191] However, all of those considerations were to 'support' decision of inventive step saying, 'Further, nonobviouness of purported invention is also supported by commercial success', or 'purported invention's commercial success alone is not enough to overturn technical obviousness of such invention'. Court case dealing with other secondary factor is not found but one case mentioning 'long-felt need and other's failure'.[192]

2. Deciding Inventive Step for Special Types of Inventions

a. New Use Invention

167. In New Use Invention of medicament, if the medicinal effect of filed invention is not easy to be inferred from known chemical structure of compounds, known components of a product, or known pharmacological mechanism, it is deemed non-obvious.[193] If the substance and field of utility of prior art and filed invention are same, 'remarkable effect' is the threshold of both novelty and inventive step.

b. Selection Invention

168. Where a selection invention generates advantageous effect in comparison with prior art, the inventive step of the selection invention can be acknowledged. In this case, all specific concepts included in the selection invention should have advantageous effects of qualitative difference or quantitative prominence.[194] The detail description of the selection invention should precisely explain what advantageous effect the invention generated in comparison with prior art. If the invention is rejected because the effect is doubted, the applicant can assert the effect concretely by submitting materials relating to experimental comparisons.[195]

---

190. Guideline, Part III, Ch. 3, 6.3.
191. Representatively, SCt. 2010. 1. 28 – 2007 Hoo 3752; SCt. 1996. 10. 11 – 96 Hoo 559.
192. SCt. 2008. 5. 29 – 2006 Hoo 3052. In the case, the inventive step of present patent was denied and the supplementary fact of 'long-felt need and other's failure' did not overturn such conclusion.
193. Examination Guidelines for Medicaments (2011), Ch. 3, 4.1.
194. SCt. 2003. 4. 25 – 2001 Hoo 2740; SCt. 2007. 9. 6 – 2005 Hoo 3338; SCt. 2010. 3. 25 – 2008 Hoo 3469, 3476.
195. SCt. 2003. 4. 25 – 2001 Hoo 2740.

c. Numeral Limitation Invention

169. Experimentally selecting an optimal numerical range from the publicly known art is normally considered as out of novelty and inventive step. However, if a limited numerical range has remarkably improved effect regarding the overall scope of the numerical limitation, the inventive step along with novelty may be acknowledged. For this: (1) the technical meaning of the numerical limitation should be described in detail, and (2) embodiments in the detail description should prove that the range of the numerical limitation is critical: that qualitatively different or quantitatively prominent effect is deprived at limited range.[196]

d. Business Method Invention

170. Business method invention is a combination of business idea and software. Thus, the standard to decide nonobviousness of BM invention may be organized as the following:

(1) Nonobvious business idea with inventive software: Highly inventive.
(2) Nonobvious business idea with normal software: Possibly inventive.
(3) Obvious business idea with inventive software: Possibly inventive.
(4) Obvious business idea with normal software: Not inventive.

II. Specification

171. Patent applicant shall submit application documents to Commissioner of KIPO, and the document shall include 'specification' consist of: (1) the title of an invention, (2) brief description of the drawings, (3) detail description of the invention, and (4) the claims.[197] Patent Act provides the requirements of claim and specification writings.[198] If those requirements are not met eventually, rejection follows[199] and invalidity for granted patent may be claimed.[200]

A. Claims

1. Sorts of Claims

172. Statutorily, two types of patent claims exist: Independent claim and Dependent claim.[201] Other practical categories of claims often discussed are the following.

196. Guideline, Part III, Ch. 3, 6.4.2.
197. PA Art. 42(2).
198. PA Art. 42(3), (4).
199. PA Art. 62. 4.
200. PA Art. 133(1) 1.
201. Presidential Decree of PA, Art. 5.

a. Functional Claim

173. The function claim refers to the claim written in the manner of 'what it does' than 'what it is'. As a claim shall specify an invention as structures, methods, functions, and materials etc.,[202] functional claim is deemed valid type of claim by statute. When functional claim is reviewed against prior art(s) in novelty and inventive step determination, the matter of claim construction arises. It is about if the functional claim shall be interpreted broadly to cover all types of possible functions, or interpreted narrowly upon the working model shown in detailed description. Supreme Court cases split into one type that reads on wordings as they are in the claim,[203] and the other type that interprets functional claim under consideration of detail description.[204] The former cases decided claims invalid, as the functional expressions encompass prior art's elements, leading the claim exposed to novelty or obviousness attacks. The later cases lead a claim to survive from prior arts, narrowing the scope of target to specific modes in descriptions.

174. On the other hand, in deciding the right's scope of granted patents, Supreme Court tends to interpret functional claim narrowly referring to specification. Consequently, the scope of right of functional claim is restricted to specific types of modes actually shown in detail descriptions.[205] In that case, another person who works claimed invention by element substantially different with those in detail description is free from infringement.

b. Product by Process Claim

175. Guideline allows this type of claim exceptionally where it is hard to explain the features of invention but by the process to produce it.[206] When deciding novelty or inventive step of product by process claim against prior art, the examiner must regard the present claim as 'product' in principle. Thus, once the same product is identified among prior arts, the novelty or inventive step of filed invention may be denied, even though the prior art's product was made in different process.[207] In the meantime, contention exists about whether the scope of patented product by process claim shall be restricted to purported process, or cover any identical product regardless of the process used. No Supreme Court's case answers to such question so far.

2. Statutory Requirements in Claim Writing

a. Support by Detail Description[208]

176. The claim shall be supported by detail description. Excessively broad claim in comparison with detail description is a claim unsupported by detail

202. PA Art. 42(6).
203. Representatively, SCt. 2005. 4. 28 – 2004 Hoo 1533; SCt. 2007. 9. 6 – 2005 Hoo 1486.
204. Representatively, SCt. 2001. 6. 29 – 98 Hoo 2252; SCt. 2006. 10. 26. – 2004 Hoo 2260.
205. SCt. 2007. 6. 14. – 200 7Hoo 883; Sct. 2008. 2. 28 – 2005 Da 77350, 77367; Sct. 2009. 4. 23. – 2009 Hoo 92. etc.
206. Guideline Part II, Ch. 4, 4.(6).
207. SCt. 2006. 6. 29 – 2004 Hoo 3416; Guideline Part III, Ch. 2, 4.1.2.(3).
208. PA Art. 42(4) 1.

description.[209] Whether the scope of claim is excessively broad or in reasonable range shall be decided in view of skilled person in the art. If it is hard for person skilled in the art to infer the technical features of claims from materials demonstrated in detail description, this standard is not met.

b. Clear and Compact Wordings[210]

177. As claims consist of words to represent the scope of right, it needs to be clear and compact. Any obscure expression needs to be excluded.

c. Provisional Application: Suspension of Claim Submission

178. When filing a patent application, any patent applicant may attach the specification without stating the scope of claims. In such cases, the specification shall be amended so as to state the claims within statutory periods.[211] This is purported as 'provisional application'. The suspended claim may be submitted within eighteen months (after that period, the invention is laid open by publication) as from filing date. If not submitted by that time, the application is deemed withdrawn.[212] In case that the applicant requests disclosure of invention before said eighteen months, he/she must submit the complete claim(s).[213]

B. Detail Description

1. Required Sufficiency and Method of Disclosure

179. In detail description: (1) field of art, (2) technical problem to be solved, (3) devised solutions of said problems, and (4) other necessary information with which person skilled in the art understand the invention, shall be included.[214] It is common view that skilled person in the art here refers to a technician with the average knowledge in the technical field to which the application belongs.[215] Supreme Court also explains that a skilled person in the art implies a person who has average technical understanding to comprehend, reproduce the invention referring to properly written descriptions.[216]

2. Applicant's Duty to Report Arts Relevant with Invention

180. Applicant is obliged to report the relevant prior art he/she referred to on the way of invention.[217] If examiner regards said obligation was not implemented

209. SCt. 2004. 12. 9 -2003 Hoo 496.
210. PA Art. 42(4) 2.
211. PA Art. 42(5).
212. PA Art 42(7).
213. PA Art. 59(2), proviso.
214. PA Art. 42(3) 2.; PA Enforcement Rule Art. 21.
215. Guideline, Part II, Ch. 3, 2.1.
216. SCt. 1999. 7. 23 – 97 Hoo 2477.
217. PA Art. 42(3) 2.

appropriately, ground for rejection shall be noticed. If applicant does not conduct proper amendment as a reaction to the notice, rejection will follow.[218]

3. Disclosure of Producing Method and Utility for Material

181. In detail description of material, the method to produce it and concrete utility of it shall be described so as to skilled person may understand. This norm is highlighted in medicament inventions, and the principle is that the claim shall consist of invented substance and its utility.[219]

4. Detail Descriptions for Special Types of Inventions

a. Selection Inventions

182. The detail description of the selection invention should precisely explain that the invention generates advantageous effect in comparison with prior art, but need not provide experimental materials to confirm the prominence of the effect (they may be submitted to attest 'inventive step' of invention when mattered).[220] Supreme Court stipulates, 'In detail description of selection invention, the technical effect and its significance that the inventor actually acknowledged should be illustrated. For this, there shall be one or more qualitative or quantitative illustration to support such significance of effect.'[221]

b. Numeral Limitation Invention

183. Supreme Court states that, 'In detail description of numeral limitation inventions, the remarkable technical effect shall be clearly illustrated by support of necessary experimental data etc. Simple statement of "outstanding effect" or "qualitatively different effect" without pertinent support is insufficient.'[222]

§4. Formality (Procedure for Grant and Obtaining Patent)

I. Principles Relevant to Patent Application

A. *First to File*

184. Where two or more applications relating to the same invention are filed on different dates, only the applicant of the earlier filing date may obtain a patent for

218. PA Art. 62. 4.; PA Art. 42(3).
219. Guideline for medicaments & cosmetics (2011) Ch. 2, 2.2.
220. Guideline, Part III, Ch. 3, 6.4.1.
221. SCt. 2009. 10. 15 – 2008 Hoo 736, 743; SCt. 2012. 8. 23 – 2010 Hoo 3424, etc.
222. SCt. 1994. 5. 13 – 93 Hoo 657; SCt. 2005. 4. 15 -2004 Hoo 448, etc.

the invention.[223] Where two or more applications relating to the same invention are filed on the same date, only the person agreed upon by all the applicants after consultation may obtain a patent for the invention. If no agreement is reached or no consultation is possible, none of the applicants shall obtain a patent for the invention.[224]

B. One Application for One Invention

185. A patent application shall relate to one invention only: Provided that a group of inventions so linked as to form a single general inventive concept may be the subject of one patent application.[225] Presidential Decree enumerates such 'link' as: (1) technical correlation between filed inventions, and (2) common technical features between filed inventions.[226]

C. Prohibition of New Matter Addition

186. An amendment to the specification or drawings shall be made within the scope of the features in the specification or drawings initially attached to the patent application.[227] Patent practice executes this doctrine of 'prohibition of new matter addition' very strictly: Amendment violating this rule leads to rejection and gives rise to claim invalidation after grant.

D. Laying-Open of Application

187. The application shall be laid open in the Patent Gazette after eighteen months from the date of filing. The application may, however, be published before the date if requested by the applicant.[228] After an application is laid open, an applicant may warn a person who has commercially or industrially used the invention, indicating that a patent application for the invention has been filed.[229] The person who used the invention after reception of warning shall remunerate patent applicant reasonable royalty after patent is granted. The period for which remuneration has to be made is from the date of warning to the date of patent registration.[230] After the registration, the use of patented invention constitutes infringement giving a rise to damages, rather than remuneration by this clause.

223. PA Art. 36(1).
224. PA Art. 36(2).
225. PA Art. 45(1).
226. PA Presidential Decree Art. 6.
227. PA Art. 47(2).
228. PA Art. 64(1).
229. PA Art. 65(1).
230. PA Art. 65(2), (3).

E. Commencement of Examination under Request

188. Applicant shall submit a request for the commencement of examination within five years as from application date.[231] Without said request, the application is deemed withdrawn.[232]

F. Examination of 'Claim By Claim' and Rejection of Whole Claims

189. Where any one of multiple claims in a single application bears reason of rejection and such reason was not overcome by the end of examination, examiner may decide rejection to whole claims.[233] Any person may assert and supply relevant information to Commissioner of KIPO to defeat the patentability of applied invention. Where the applicant has received a decision to reject a patent application, applicant may request a trial of appeal within thirty days as from the date when such decision is noticed.[234]

II. Amendment

A. Amendment in General

190. Applicant may amend the specification any time before delivering a certified copy of a decision to grant a patent. However, the prohibition of new matter addition is strictly applied to amendment. If the amendment is a reaction to examiner's office action other than voluntary one, gradually stricter limitations for substance, timing, and number are imposed by the law.[235]

B. Divisional Application

191. As a special type of amendment, applicant may divide initial application into two or more applications. Divisional application is permissible only within the contents of initial specification and drawings, and procedural time limitation entails.[236] Divided application is deemed applied as such on the date of initial application.

231. PA Art. 59(2).
232. PA Art. 59(5).
233. Guideline, Part V, Ch. 3, 12.2. (4); Sct. 1993. 9. 14 – 92 Hoo 1615.
234. PA Art. 132-3.
235. PA Art. 47(1), (3).
236. PA Art. 52(1).

C. Converted Application

192. Applicant may covert initial application of utility model into a patent or initial application of patent into a utility model, choosing advantageous type of right for obtaining or management.[237] Converted application is also permissible only within the contents of initial specification and drawings, and procedural time limitation entails.[238] Converted application is deemed applied as such on the date of initial application.

III. Application with Priority Claim

A. Priority Claim under Treaty

193. Being a Member State of Paris Convention, Patent Act provides application with priority claim under treaty.[239] A person eligible for making a priority claim under the treaty is a national of a State party to the treaty or a national of a non-State party who has a domicile or a real and effective industrial or commercial establishment in a State party. The State parties include the Member States of the Paris Convention and the WTO.[240] The period allowed for filing an application claiming a priority under the Paris Convention shall be within one year from the filing date of the initial application filed in one of the countries under the Treaty.[241]

B. Application with Domestic Priority Claim

194. Applicant who made follow-up invention that encompasses formerly applied invention may claim 'domestic priority' based upon former invention. In this case, the filing date of overlapping parts with formerly applied invention retroacts to former application date, while there is no retroactive effect of filing date for newly added matter(s).[242] Domestic priority claim is designed to ensure protection for an invention, which has been improved from or added to the prior application. Without this rule, where an invention which specified, improved, or enlarged prior invention is filed in an ordinary patent filing process, such invention may be rejected due to lack of novelty or inventive step against applied invention. Normal amendment of prior specification reflecting new invention shall trigger new matter addition rule due to extra elements added to prior invention. Domestic priority claim prevents such irrationality and protects serial inventions, which are the outcomes of technological development of single inventor.[243] The domestic priority claim shall be made within one year as from initial application.

237. PA Art. 53.
238. PA Art. 53(1).
239. PA Art. 54.
240. Guideline Part VI, Ch. 3, 3.1.
241. PA Art. 54(1).
242. PA Art. 55.
243. Guideline Part VI, Ch. 4, 2.

§5. Ownership and Transfer (Assignment: Licenses)

I. Right to Obtain Patent

A. Initial Entitlement of Right

195. Inventor is entitled to obtain patent.[244] Where invention is made by co-operation, the co-inventors enjoy joint ownership of right to obtain patent.[245] Where the right to obtain a patent is jointly owned, all the owners shall jointly file a patent application.[246]

B. Successor of Right

196. As the right to obtain patent is deemed a property right, it is transferrable.[247] Legitimate successor of such right may file for patent in his/her name.[248] It is to be noted that the aforesaid legitimacy of successor's application does 'not' mean the successor may indicate himself/herself as the inventor.

II. Derivation

A. Definition

197. Derivation refers to the discordance between the holder of right to obtain patent and patent applicant. Derivation exists: (1) where a third party who has no right to obtain patent (neither an inventor nor a successor of right) files for patent in his/her name, (2) where a part of joint inventor(s) file for patent leaving other joint inventor(s) out. Supreme Court adjudicated, 'Where a third party converted the components of original invention before application, it is still derivation of said invention if the conversion is no more than addition, deletion or substitution of equivalents, causing no significant improvement of technical effect.'[249]

B. Legal Effect of Derivation

198. No merit as prior application is conferred on derived invention; the later application of legitimate right holder is uninfluenced by first to file doctrine, as the deriver's application is no prior application at all.[250] Derivation leads to rejection

244. PA Art. 33(1).
245. PA Art. 33(2).
246. PA Art. 44.
247. PA Art. 37.
248. PA Art. 33(1); PA Art. 42(1) 1.
249. SCt, 2011. 9. 29 – 2009 Hoo 2463.
250. PA Art. 36(5).

and invalidation of granted patent.[251] Once application is finally rejected due to derivation, the right holder's application which intervenes between derived application and said confirmed rejection retroacts to filing date of deriver's application.[252] Consequently, the right holder succeeds procedural state of application formed by deriver. Similarly, once a granted patent is invalidated due to derivation, the right holder's application which intervenes between derived application and said confirmed invalidation retroacts to filing date of deriver's.[253] However, this shall not apply where right holder's application is filed more than two years after the deriver's patent grant or more than thirty days after invalidation.

To sum up, the right holder must file for patent himself/herself to obtain patent. On the other side, the right holder may have deriver's application rejected or invalidated and exploit the procedural state of deriver's in retroactive manner for his/her subsequent application.

III. Employee's Invention

A. *Entitlement of Patent for Employee's Invention*

199. Principally, the right to obtain patent for employee's work belongs to employee (inventor),[254] whereas the right goes to government once invention is made by government employee.[255] Where employee obtains patent for employee's invention, employer obtains statutory license free of charge for that patent, which is effective to third party without registration.[256]

B. *Succession of Right by Employer*

200. Employer may succeed the right to obtain a patent from employee by contract. The succession comes into force with employer's notices to employer.[257] Where employer succeeded employee's right, he/she bears obligation of due remuneration.[258] The rate of remuneration is decided considering total proportion of contribution to the invention. This is because employee's invention is possible on employer's supply of fund, facility, or manpower. In practice, many employers refrain from succession of right from employee, which brings duty of compensation. It may be profitable enough for them to enjoy statutory license allowed free. This sometimes leads employees, who have no capability to practice patented invention, to situation of no reward for their endeavour. Recently, Promotion of

251. PA Art. 62; 133(1).
252. PA Art. 34.
253. PA Art. 35.
254. Promotion of Invention Act, Art. 10(1).
255. Promotion of Invention Act, Art. 10(2).
256. Promotion of Invention Act, Art. 10(1).
257. Promotion of Invention Act, Art. 13(2).
258. Promotion of Invention Act, Art. 15(1).

Invention Act has been amended to cope with this situation, urging major companies to succeed employee's invention.[259]

201. The prior consent to transfer the right to obtain patent for private inventions of employee to employer shall be deemed void.[260] This is to prevent employer, the stronger party in employment contract, from exploiting employee with unbalanced contract clause.

C. *Calculation of Due Remuneration*

202. The employee who considers the remuneration from employer unduly small may bring a suit against employer to seek for payment of the difference. However, it is to be noted that whole amount of profit the employer earned from the invention shall not be the ground to calculate due remunerations. The employer may use the invention free under statutory license; thus, certain portion of profit from the invention must be allocated to employer as initial value. Such amount shall be deducted from total profit and employee's remuneration is calculated upon the rest amount of money. In addition, the ground profits of remuneration are limited to profits sourced from employer's exclusive right as patent holder: profits from the status of licensor, or exclusive use of patented invention. Thus, where employer, as patentee of employee's invention, reaped royalty from the third party, such will be ground profit to be remunerated as it is.

IV. Establishment of Patent Right

203. Patent right is established with registration. Once decision of grant is confirmed, applicant shall pay registration fee. Commissioner of the KIPO shall register the establishment of a patent right where the payment of patent fees has been made.[261] Commissioner shall publish the grant of the patent together with the relevant information in the Patent Gazette.[262]

V. Transfer

A. *Transfer and Establishment of Pledge*

204. Patent right is transferrable. The transfer of patent right shall be registered to take effect.[263] Where patent right is joint-owned, the share may be transferred under unanimous agreement of all joint owners. It is the same when a joint owner wants to give a license to third party for the patented invention.[264] On the other

259. Promotion of Invention Act, Art. 10(1) 1.
260. Promotion of Invention Act, Art. 10(3).
261. PA Art. 87(2).
262. PA Art. 87(3).
263. PA Art. 99(1); Art. 101.
264. PA Art. 99(2), (4).

hand, any joint owner may use the patented invention entirely without consent of other joint owner(s).[265] Joint owner bears no obligation to share the profit from such individual use to other joint owner(s).

B. License

1. Exclusive License

205. Patent right holder may set exclusive license, which subsists with registration.[266] Exclusive licensee has a right to use the invention exclusively within the scope set by contract. Patent right holder cannot give third party another license overlapping with prior exclusive license, and licensor cannot use the licensed invention himself/herself. Exclusive license is an in rem right to exclude others; therefore, the licensee may seek for remedies against infringers in his/her name.[267] Patent Act provides equivalent protections to exclusive licensee with patent right holder.[268] In contrast with old Patent Act, current Act qualifies exclusive licensee as a plaintiff of Trial to Confirm Scope of Right as with patent right holder.[269]

2. Non-exclusive License

206. Non-exclusive license is a contractual right to claim licensor not to exercise patent right against use of invention. Due to the nature as contractual right, non-exclusive licensee cannot seek for remedies against infringer in his/her name. Instead, licensee can only demand licensor to exercise injunctive right against infringer for licensee's sake. Further, licensee shall not claim right to a third party who was assigned of patent right or obtained exclusive license, i.e., in rem rights. However, once licensee registered the right, it may be claimed against those parties.[270] Non-exclusive license is generally set by contract. Still, there are various cases of non-exclusive license and compulsory license set by statute or government order.

§6. Scope of Exclusive Rights

I. Working of Patented Invention and All Elements Rule

207. A patentee shall have the exclusive right to work a patented invention commercially and industrially.[271] The working of invention refers to:[272]

---

265. PA Art. 99(3).
266. PA Art. 100(1).
267. PA Art. 128(1).
268. PA Art. 126 through Art. 132.
269. PA Art. 135(1).
270. PA Art. 118(1).
271. PA Art. 94.
272. PA Arts 2. 3.

(1) In cases of product invention, acts of manufacturing, using, assigning, leasing, importing, or offering for assigning or leasing the product.
(2) In cases of process invention, acts of using the process.
(3) In cases of an invention of a process to manufacture a product, acts of using, assigning, leasing, importing, or offering for assigning or leasing the product manufactured by the process, in addition to the acts mentioned in (2).

208. Any act of working patented invention without right holder's consent constitutes infringement. Multiple components and organization of such components constitute claimed invention as a whole. Thus, infringement occurs only where every element of claimed invention is worked, and if any element in claim is missing in working, it is not infringement (All Elements Rule).

II. Principles of Claim Interpretation

A. *Literal Interpretation*

209. The principle of literal interpretation implies: (1) the expressions in claim shall be interpreted by their literal meaning of vocabulary to assure objectiveness and predictability, (2) what was unwritten in the claim shall not be considered as element of claim, regardless that it is expressed in detailed description or drawings. This is because the scope of patent right is determined by elements in claim and the demerits from omission shall be returned to applicant (patent holder).

B. *Consideration of Detail Description*

210. Where meaning of claim is ambiguous only with literal interpretation, it may be clarified by considering detail description.[273] A judge shall not narrow meaning of claimed words referring to detail description as long as the meaning of word in claim is clear by itself. The disadvantage that the claim is defeated by prior art due to its wideness shall go to patent holder. As patent holder would enjoy wide range of right against third parties thanks to that wide claim, it has a nature of 'double-edged sword'. Thus, a judge shall not arbitrarily read in detail description to define meaning of claimed expression unless it is 'ambiguous'.

C. *Consideration of Prosecution History*

211. If the applicant has asserted in examination procedure that his/her claim shall be interpreted narrowly to secure patentability, such history shall be considered where the patent holder exercises his/her right against third party after he/she obtained patent. Consequently, the scope of pertinent claim shall be interpreted

273. SCt. 2009. 10. 15 – 2009 Da 19925; SCt. 2008. 7. 10 – 2008 Hoo 64, etc.

narrowly along with patent holder's assertion in prosecution.[274] This is a kind of estoppels in patent right. Supreme Court also said, 'Where the applicant received office action pointing out defect of detail description and inventive step and narrowed his claim by amendment to avoid rejection, the part left shall be deemed abandoned by applicant.'[275]

III. Substance of Exclusive Right of Patent

212. Exclusive right of patent comprises of:

(1) Right to work patented invention.
(2) Right to give license to other.
(3) Right to prohibit infringer from working the invention.
(4) Right to seek for damages, return of unjust enrichment and recovery of reputation against infringer.

(1) and (2) were already described above, and (3), (4) will be described in § 9.

§7. Limitations and Exceptions to the Scope of Patent Protection: Compulsory License, Etc.

I. Statutory/Compulsory Licenses

A. Non-exclusive License for Prior User

213. At the time of patent application, if a person, who has made an invention separately or obtained the substance of invention from such person, has been working the invention commercially or industrially in Korea in good faith, he/she shall have a non-exclusive license on that patent.[276] This is an exceptional rule of first to file doctrine, to rescue prior inventor and his/her business in good faith. The statutory licensee of prior user right need not pay any royalty and the license is effective to third party without registration.[277]

B. Non-exclusive License for Business Based upon Double Patent

214. Where double patent was granted for identical invention, any person who has begun business or its preparation based on such patent in good faith, shall obtain statutory license regardless that the patent he/she relied on became invalid.[278] This

274. SCt. 2003. 12. 12 – 2002 Hoo 2181, etc.
275. SCt. 2008. 4. 10 – 2006 Da 35308.
276. PA Art. 103.
277. PA Art. 118(2).
278. PA Art. 104(1).

doctrine is to protect a party who trusted validity of registered patent and made business investment on that fair trust. This type of statutory licensee shall pay royalty to patent owner.[279]

C. *Compulsory Licenses*

1. Expropriation of Patent Rights

215. If a patented invention is necessary for national defence in time of war, uprising, or any other similar emergency, the government may expropriate a patent right.[280] With the expropriation, all rights other than patent extinct.[281] Government shall pay fair remuneration to patent owner and lawful licensee.[282] Expropriation of patent is exercised by Commissioner of KIPO under request of relevant government cabinet Minister.

2. Working of Patented Invention by Government, Etc.

216. If it is deemed necessary to work a patented invention non-commercially due to a national or extreme emergency, or for the public interests, the Government may directly work the patented invention or have any person work it.[283] Fair remuneration shall follow to patent holder or lawful licensee for this working.[284]

3. Adjudication for Grant of Non-exclusive License

217. Where a patented invention falls under any of the following, and where agreement is not reached while having a consultation with the patentee or where the consultation is unable to take place, a person who intends to work the patented invention may request the Commissioner of KIPO to adjudicate for grant of a non-exclusive license:[285]

(1) Where the patented invention has not been worked for three or more consecutive years in Korea, except in cases of natural disaster, unavoidable circumstances or other justifiable reasons prescribed by Presidential Decree.
(2) Where the patented invention has not been continuously worked commercially or industrially in Korea on a substantial scale during a period of three or more

279. PA Art. 104(2).
280. PA Art. 106(1).
281. PA Art. 106(2).
282. PA Art. 106(3).
283. PA Art. 106-2(1).
284. PA Art. 106-2(3).
285. PA Art. 107.

years without justifiable grounds, or where the demand in Korea for the patented invention has not been satisfied to an appropriate extent and under reasonable conditions.

(3) Where the working of the patented invention is especially necessary for public interests.
(4) Where the working of the patented invention is necessary to remedy judicially confirmed unfair competition deeds.
(5) Where the working of the patented invention is necessary for exporting medicines to countries intending to import the medicines to cure diseases that threaten the health of the majority of its citizens.

The adjudication for grant of non-exclusive license mainly matters with pharmaceutical inventions. In Korea, the provision to entitle compulsory license for pharmaceutical patents is Article 107. 3. However, no case that compulsory license was adjudicated over patented pharmaceutical products has been reported so far in Korea.

4. Trial for Granting Non-exclusive License

218. If a patented invention is an 'incremental invention', the work of which inevitably entails work of other's prior patent, and the patentee of prior invention refuses license without justifiable grounds or it is impossible to obtain such permission, the patentee of incremental invention may bring up a trial for the grant of a non-exclusive license.[286] Such non-exclusive license shall be granted only where the incremental invention brings important technical advance having substantial economical value in comparison with prior invention.[287] If the patentee-granting license by the trial needs to work the incremental invention, he/she may counter claim non-exclusive license for aforesaid incremental patent.[288] In either case, the licensee shall pay or deposit reasonable royalty before working.

II. Limitations on Patent Rights: Experimental Use Etc.

219. The effects of the patent right shall not extend to the followings:[289]

(1) Working of the patented invention for the purpose of research or experiments, including where such experiments are done on pharmaceutical or agrochemical items for pertinent permission of health authority or reporting for commercialization.
(2) Vessels, aircraft or vehicles merely passing through Korea, or machinery, instruments, equipment or other accessories used therein.

286. PA Art. 138(1).
287. PA Art. 138(2).
288. PA Art. 138(3).
289. PA Art. 96.

(3) Articles existing in Korea at the time the patent application is filed.

The patent right, for a medicine manufactured by mixing two or more medicines, or for processes of manufacturing medicines by mixing two or more medicines, shall not extend to the acts of manufacturing medicines or to medicines manufactured by such acts where such manufacture is done by authentic pharmacist.[290]

§8. Duration of Protection: Maintaining and Termination of Patent Protection

I. Duration of Patent Right

220. The right of granted patent subsists twenty years as from its filing date.[291] Where the regulation requires additional permit of government or registration before working patented invention, and takes a long time due to activity or safety tests, the duration period of patent right may be extended up to five years corresponding to such delay.[292] The period, which has lapsed due to patentee, shall not be included in such extension. Where a patent is granted four years after application or three years after request of examination (the later date of either becomes standard), duration period of granted patent shall be extended corresponding to delayed period. The patentee who seeks for this extension shall prosecute statutory process.[293]

II. Fees, Extinction, and Abandonment of Patent Right

221. Any person to register granted patent shall pay fee of three years at once. As from the fourth year after registration, the fee shall be paid annually.[294] Failing of fee payment leads to extinction of granted patent.[295] Patentee may abandon patent right and such patent extinct immediately.[296]

§9. Infringement and Remedies

I. Infringements

222. Where a person works all elements in patented claim, infringement occurs. The types of infringement recognized by practice and court cases are as followings.

290. PA Art. 96(2).
291. PA Art. 88(1).
292. PA Art. 89(1).
293. PA Art. 92-2.
294. PA Art. 79.
295. PA Art. 81(3).
296. PA Art. 120.

A. *Literal Infringement*

223. Literal infringement is recognized where each and every element of unpermitted working falls 'element by element' on patented claim. Consequently, if any element of claimed invention is missing in working invention, it is not literal infringement at least.

B. *Equivalent Infringement*

1. Definition

224. Equivalent infringement refers to a situation that one or more elements of working invention is not identical with claimed invention but such difference is deemed equivalent with claimed elements (Doctrine of Equivalents). Doctrine of equivalents extends the scope of patented claim out of its literal range for 'substantial protection' of patentee, and makes an exception to All Elements Rule. In the meantime, doctrine of equivalents may harm the objectiveness and predictability of infringement, legal stability of third parties, which are original and integral functions of claim. However, the doctrine has been taken for granted to prevent infringers from abusing all elements rule. Otherwise, they can deviate from infringement by simply altering non-substantial element(s) of claimed invention, enjoying almost every technical effect of patented invention.

2. Requirements

225. 'SCt. 2000. 7. 28 – 97 Hoo 2200' is the leading case of doctrine of equivalence in Korea, and series of Supreme Court's cases have followed. The case stipulated that infringement occurs even where the infringer substitutes some elements of claimed invention, where following conditions are met.

a. Identity of Principle Technical Solution

226. This condition implies the main components of both inventions are substantially same, and fundamental parts of patented elements are appropriated by the infringer. Supreme Court recently remarked: 'The identity of principle technical solution means that the substituted element is insubstantial component of patented invention; both inventions are still in common in light of features as a whole despite of the missing part,' and 'such decision shall be based upon the view of skilled person in the art and total sense of specification'.[297]

297. SCt. 2009. 12. 24. -2007 Da 66422; SCt. 2011. 5. 26. – 2010 Da 75839.

b. Possibility of Substitution

227. This requirement implies that the second invention still brings substantially same technical effect with original invention. This is natural requirement as the infringer should be able to enjoy substantially same technical effect after taking equivalent alteration of element(s).

c. Obviousness of Substitution

228. To establish equivalent infringement, the substitution of element shall be 'obvious' to a person skilled in the art. The obviousness here must be clear and convincing than the obviousness in deciding inventive step. If the substitution is not 'highly obvious' among skilled person in the art, it is not estimated as simple adoption of equivalents. Otherwise, interpretation shall allow patentee excessive protection to control other's lawful technical discretion. With regard to this requirement, the timing standard to decide obviousness may play integral role. If the standard is set on application date, substitution may not be obvious to person skilled in the art, whereas, if the standard is set on when infringement occurs, the substitution shall be more obvious to a person skilled in the art, leading to equivalent infringement. This is because technical capacity of person skilled in the art tends to increase with lapse of time.

d. Exclusion of Art in Public Domain

229. Where the alleged infringer is simply working arts in public domain, the patentee is not allowed to claim equivalent infringement over such a work. If the patented invention itself is 'almost' in public domain, giving a rise to invalidation issue, it is inappropriate to extend the scope of such problematic right in the name of equivalence.

e. Consideration of Prosecution History

230. 'Consideration of Prosecution History' estops patentee from asserting his/her right in contradictorily manner with prosecution history. If the applicant has shrunk the scope of patent claim to go through prosecution, it is often unfair trying to recoup that scope of right he/she abandoned under name of equivalents after procuring right.

C. Infringement by Incremental Invention

231. Infringement by incremental invention occurs where a third party who works his/her invention, which encompasses every element of formerly patented invention incrementally improving it.[298] Even if the incremental invention

298. SCt. 1991. 11. 26 – 90 Hoo 1499.

substituted some elements of prior invention as equivalents, it does not bring any difference in infringement.[299]

232. Large portion of modern inventions are incremental inventions. It is even general trend in some field of technology (e.g., IT and software). One may obtain patent for incremental invention utilizing other's patented invention, whether there was permission or not. However, the later invention may not be worked without consent of former invention's patentee, as it inevitably entails infringement of former invention. To cope with the situation that former patent unjustly obstruct the use of its incremental invention patent and frustrate technological improvements, Patent Act provides a 'Trial for Granting Non-Exclusive License' for patentee of incremental invention.[300] However, such non-exclusive license shall be granted only where the incremental invention brings important technical advance having substantial economical value in comparison with prior invention. This is a rule to balance the interest of former patentee and interest of incremental invention's patentee along with public concern of technological innovation.

D. *Special Type of Incremental Invention: Selection Invention*

233. As aforementioned, the chemical invention of sub-range substance, which brings about quantitatively or qualitatively outstanding effect in comparison with known larger-range substance, i.e., selection invention, is patentable. In contrast with its patentability, whether the work of patented selection invention constitutes infringement is questioned. This is because the work of selection invention naturally accompanies the use of formerly patented invention (the larger-range substance). To this issue, Supreme Court purported, where an invention is patented as selection invention, its use is not an infringement of larger-range substance patent.[301]

E. *Deeds Regarded as Infringement (Indirect Infringement)*

1. Statute

234. Patent Act Article 127 provides any of the following deeds as business shall be deemed infringement:

(1) In cases of product invention, acts of making, assigning, leasing, importing, or offering for assignment or lease articles used exclusively for producing invented products.
(2) In cases of the invention of process, acts of making, assigning, leasing, importing or offering for assignment or lease articles used exclusively for working invented process.

---

299. SCt. 2001. 9.7 – 2001 Hoo 393.
300. PA Art. 98; PA Art. 138.
301. SCt. 1991. 11. 12 – 90 Hoo 960.

Namely, this is about 'indirect infringement' of patent right. Indirect infringement provision prohibits certain act of 'physical aid' to direct infringement, in order to protect patent right effectively.[302]

2. Requirements to Constitute Indirect Infringement

235. Indirect infringement occurs only for the supply of 'non-staple goods (the goods that is used exclusively)' for producing patented products or working invented process. Thus, the supply of general-purpose goods arouses no indirect infringement issue even where it is used for direct infringement. In practice, establishment of indirect infringement is often pertinent to 'reproduction' and 'repair'. For the patented item lawfully sold, the 'exhaustion of patent right' occurs. Thus, if the owner of such item repairs it, it is lawful exercise of ownership and not infringement. However, if the degree of repair is so excessive to be regarded as 'reproduction', exhaustion rule does not work and infringement occurs. To be noted, only the works of patented invention 'as business' constitutes infringement in Korea;[303] therefore, only the property owner who reproduce the item as business is patent infringer. Nonetheless, the indirect infringement can be established for aiding private reproduction (infringement) as long as supplying non-staple goods to such fair reproduction are done as business.

236. The relation among said legal elements can be summed up as the following:

(1) If the property owner merely repairs patented item, he/she is not infringer at all and no indirect infringement steps in.
(2) If the property owner reproduces patented item as business, he/she is direct infringer and the acts of physical aid (making, assigning, leasing, importing, or offering for assignment or lease articles used exclusively for such production) constitutes indirect infringement.
(3) If the property owner reproduces patented item for private purpose, he/she is not infringer, while the provider of foresaid type of physical aid as business is still indirect infringer. Considering it is a general rule of torts in Korea that establishment of direct infringement is prerequisite of indirect infringement, this is a statutory exception of such a tort rule.

With respect to replacement of component, Supreme Court adjudicated, 'In the event that 1) patentee supplies expendable component of patented item in the market; 2) it is a business scheme of patentee to sell those component as "repair unit"; 3) the component has no other use but for patented item, the act to sale said component without permission constitutes indirect infringement.'[304]

302. SCt. 2009. 9. 10 – 2007 Hoo 3356.
303. PA Art. 94.
304. SCt. 2001. 1. 30 – 98 Hoo 2580.

3. Remedies for Indirect Infringement

237. Patentee may seek for prohibition order against indirect infringer.[305] Due to the features as in rem remedies, prohibition order against indirect infringer may be ordered regardless of wilfulness or negligence. Damages are also available against indirect infringement of wilfulness or negligence. Patentee may lead indirect infringer to such subjective condition by warning. On the other side, with regard to possibility of criminal sanction against indirect infringement, Supreme Court takes negative position.[306]

II. Defences against Infringement Allegation

238. Defendant in patent infringement suit may primarily submit defence of contractual or statutory license, limitation of patent right, exhaustion, etc. The followings are other significant defences ordinarily submitted in practice.

A. Invalidity of Patent

239. Supreme Court has decided that defendant may argue the invalidity of patent on the ground of novelty, insufficient disclosure, first to file doctrine, etc. For whether the defendant may argue patent's invalidity on the ground of obviousness, Supreme Court was negative. The logic of Supreme Court for such stance was that nonobviouness is a hard question for infringement suit judge to determine, and such shall be resolved in invalidation process of expertise, i.e., trial at KIPO and subsequent appeal in Patent Court. However, Supreme Court changed its position through late en banc decision, allowing every cause of invalidation including obviousness as defence in infringement suit. Now Supreme Court regards exercising patent right where its invalidity is apparent, as 'Abuse of Right'.[307]

B. Arts in Public Domain

240. Conventionally, courts have allowed defence of 'Arts in Public Domain' in infringement suit. If an art identical with patented invention was publicly known before its filing date, defendant may argue his work is mere use of arts in public domain other than patented invention. Extensional argument was allowed where all components of patented invention had been in public domain and it was easy for person skilled in the art to combine those elements leading to identical arts with patented invention. Substantially, the former is close to invalidation defence based upon lack of novelty, and the latter is defence based upon lack of inventive step.

305. PA Art. 126.
306. SCt. 1993. 2. 23 – 92 Do 3350.
307. SCt. 2012. 1. 19 – 2010 Da 95390.

C. Unfair Competition

241. Article 59 of Monopoly Regulation and Unfair Trade Act stipulates, 'This Act shall not apply to any act which is deemed the justifiable exercise of the right under the Copyright Act, the Patent Act, the Utility Model Act, the Design Protection Act or the Trademark Act.' With reverse interpretation of this clause, the 'unjustifiable' exercises of patent right is under control of said Monopoly Regulation and Unfair Trade Act. Further, the right holder shall be imposed of damages along with the order of correction in such cases.

The representative examples of unjustifiable patent exercises in anti-competition law's aspect are: (1) to abuse market-dominant position by unfairly denying transaction, discriminating against certain transaction partner (e.g., failure of FRAND: Fair, Reasonable, and Non-discriminative)commitment); (2) to deter licensee from purchasing competitor' goods; (3) to restrict transaction partner, purchasing source of materials, retail price, etc. Fair Trade Commission provides the 'Examination Guidelines for Unfair Exercise of Intellectual Property Rights' enumerating further detailed examples of patent right abuse in light of unfair competition law. In those cases, the defendant may argue plaintiff's exercise of patent right shall be deterred as it is anti-competitive acts, falling on 'abuse of right'.

III. Remedies

242. In light of remedies, Patent Act confers equivalent power on exclusive licensee of patent. Accordingly, the expression of 'patent right holder' or 'patentee' below implies 'the owner of patent right holder and exclusive licensee'.

A. Prohibition Order (Injunction)

243. As aforementioned, the liability from direct infringement may be held even without wilfulness or negligence of infringer. Prohibition order is the most influential and instant remedy against infringement. Article 126 provides:

(1) Patent right holder may demand infringer to suspend such act; may demand a person likely to infringe to take preventive measures.
(2) Patent right holder may also demand infringer to abandon the objects made by infringement.

Further, prohibition may be ordered in form of provisional disposition, which may be rendered with plaintiff's vindication of 'right to be preserved' and 'necessity of preservation' under Part 4. of Civil Execution Act. Such provisional type of prohibition is threatening enough to defendant as it practically deters him/her from business for substantial period time.

244. There are discussions to put prohibition order under 'discretion' of courts other than automatic rendering, while damages are assured unlimitedly against patent infringement. Initially, said discussions were introduced to control Patent Trolls, which tends to abuse prohibition order as leverage of money making negotiations. Recently, such discussion is extended to the cases that: (1) pertinent patent license is unachieved despite of strong public needs, (2) the object of patent is a component of whole item and patentee refuses to allow a license, obstructing use of whole item, (3) prohibition is abused as a measures of enforcing unfair trade, or (4) the patentee demands prohibition while the invalidity of a patent is clear, etc. This situation reflects the recognition of necessity to control prohibition power of patent to prevent its possible side effects.

B. Damages

245. Infringement of patent right is an act of 'tort'. Damages are available to torts of wilfulness or negligence in accordance with relevant provisions in Civil Act.[308] However, in most cases, it is hard for plaintiff to prove causal relation between infringement and actual damages. To alleviate this problem and protect plaintiff effectively, Patent Act provides several special articles of damage calibration rules, which are based upon some legal presumptions.

1. 'Number of Transferred Articles by Infringer' X 'Profit per Unit of Right Holder'[309]

246. In measuring damages, the amount of loss may be calculated by multiplying 'the number of articles infringer transferred' by 'the right holder's possible profit per unit of the article'. In such cases, the compensation shall be determined between the amount that right holder's total capability of sales would have produced as maximum, and the amount that right holder has sold actually under circumstance of infringement. Where defendant successfully attests the amount that plaintiff would not have obtained even without infringement, such amount shall be deducted from aforesaid damage amount. The burden of proof for such special facts to overturn statutory presumption goes to defendant.

2. Presumption of Infringer's Profit to Damages

247. If infringer has gained any profit by infringement, the relevant amount of profit shall be presumed to be the amount of damages sustained by patent right holder.[310] As with Article 128(1), this provision is regarded applicable only where patent right holder produces or sales patented articles by himself/herself.[311] Whereas

308. Civil Act, Art. 750.
309. PA Art. 128(1).
310. PA Art. 128(2).
311. SCt. 2006. 10. 12 – 2006 Da 1831.

the structure of provision seems more straightforward than Article 128(1), it is generally hard for plaintiff to prove 'profit' of defendant.

3. Reasonable Royalty

248. Plaintiff may choose the amount of reasonable royalty as damages for patent infringement.[312] This provision is applicable regardless whether patent right holder produces or sales patented articles by himself/herself or not. Deciding damages by Article 128(1) or (2), the court may exercise its discretion to deduct where it was not wilful infringement or of gross negligence. In contrast with it, there is no space of discretion and the reasonable royalty works as minimum guarantee of damages for every infringement. The 'reasonable royalty' here denotes objective amount of money, which would have been paid if infringer had gone into a license contract with right holder. If any case of prior license exists, the actual amount of royalty may be standard; if no such case exists, the practical royalty in the field of work will be criteria deciding reasonable royalty.[313]

4. Decision of Damages by Discretion

249. Where it is difficult to decide damages by Article 128(1) through (3), court may fix considerable damages on its discretion in the light of total purport and evidence in litigation.[314] This is supplemental rule provided for plaintiff who evidently suffered damages by infringement but eventually failed to prove any of its amounts.

C. Return of Unjust Enrichment

250. Patent right holder may seek for 'return of unjust enrichment' caused by infringement selectively with damages. The option of return of unjust enrichment is merited for plaintiff in light of extinctive prescription (long term of ten years, while that of damages is short term of three years). On the other hand, there is no applicability of presumption rules of Article 128; plaintiff bears heavy burden of proof for causation between infringement and defendant's enrichment.

D. Recovery of Reputation

251. Upon request of a right holder, court may order the infringer who has injured the business reputation of right holder to take necessary measures to restore

312. PA Art. 128(3).
313. SCt. 2006. 4. 27 – 2003 Da 15006.
314. PA Art. 128(5).

the business reputation of right holder.[315] Typically, the harm of reputation is caused by low quality of infringing articles. The representative measure to restore business reputation is to publish the fact of infringement on newspaper, magazine, etc.

E. Other Provisions to Support Damages Remuneration

1. Presumption of Process of Manufacturing

252. Where a patent has been granted to an invention of a process for manufacturing a product, any product identical to the said product shall be presumed to have been manufactured by the patented process. In such cases, defendant bears burden of proof that such product was manufactured in process other than plaintiff's process.[316]

2. Presumption of Negligence

253. A person who has infringed a patent right of another person shall be presumed to have been negligent regarding such act of infringement.[317]

3. Submission Order of Documents

254. In litigation relating to the infringement of a patent right, the court may, upon request of a party, order the other party to submit documents necessary for the assessment of losses caused by the infringement: Provided that this shall not apply when the person possessing the documents has a justifiable ground for refusing to submit them.[318]

IV. Criminal Sanctions

255. In Korea, patent infringements are subject to criminal sanctions of imprisonment or fine. As for a representative example, any person who infringes a patent right shall be punished by imprisonment not exceeding seven years or by a fine not exceeding KRW 100 million.[319] Penalties paired with individual types of infringement are provided in Article 225 through Article 229.

315. PA Art. 131.
316. PA Art. 129.
317. PA Art. 130.
318. PA Art. 132.
319. PA Art. 225.

V. Protection of Trade Secret in Patent Litigations

256. Where trade secret is endangered to be revealed in the process of litigation, the party may seek for measure to protect secret vindicating such situations to the court. The court shall order pertinent parties who became to know the secret through litigation process to take appropriate measures to preserve such secret.[320]

§10. Overlapping and Relation to Other Intellectual Property Laws

257. Patent Act functions as a model law of Utility Models Act, Design Protection Act, Plant Variety Act, and Semiconductor Act, which apply many of substantial or procedural rules of Patent Act *mutatis mutandis*. For the detail, relevant explanations in each Act shall be referred to.

§11. Patent Trial and Patent Litigation

258. Patent litigation in Korea follows double tracks. This bifurcated process may be illustrated as below.

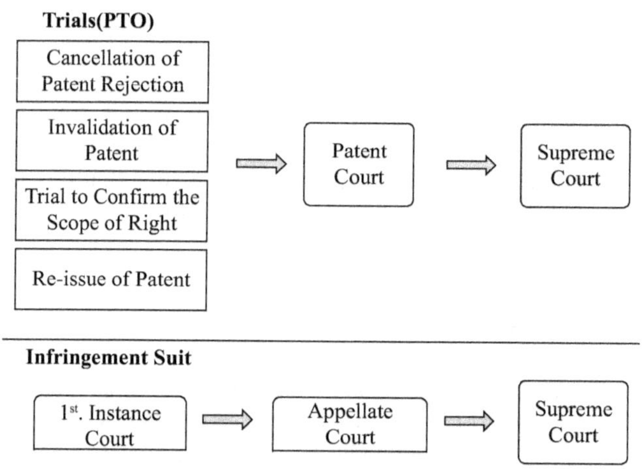

I. Patent Infringement Litigation

259. Patent infringement litigation belongs to civil procedure. The jurisdiction of litigation is disposed to civil courts. Sole judge or three-panel body of district court adjudicates according to value of lawsuit. Appeal for the first instance decision of sole judge is disposed to appellate body of district court, while the appeal

320. PA Art. 224-3.

for the decision of three-panel body of district court is in charge of high court where the district court belongs to. Supreme Court exercises jurisdiction of final appeal, which concentrates on matter of law. The legal principles described in § 9 are those applied in infringement litigations. In infringement litigation, the burdens to have judges understand substance of pertinent technology is at each party. Meanwhile, court may get assistance from expert witness to understand technology.

260. In addition to infringement suit, which mainly comprise of prohibition and damages, provisional disposition (preliminary injunction) also plays significant role in practice. The biggest merit of provisional disposition is its promptness in comparison with judgment on the merits. For that reason, court generally orders deposit for provisional order to secure and compensate possible damages of defendant. For provisional disposition: (1) the right and probability of its infringement, and (2) imminent necessity of preservation shall be vindicated.

II. Patent Trial and Appeal to Patent Court

261. The other group of patent litigation is patent trials at tribunal board of KIPO and its appeal to Patent Court. Tribunal board in KIPO exercises first instance jurisdiction over patent related trials described below. The panels are KIPO officers and most of them have careers as examiners. Tribunal is conducted by three panel members and its proceeding is quite similar to judicial procedures.

A. *Patent Trials*

1. Trial against Rejection to Application

262. When an applicant has received a decision of rejection or revocation from an examiner, applicant may demand an appeal to tribunal board within thirty days after he/she received notification.[321]

2. Invalidation Trial

263. Any interested party or examiner may bring up invalidation trial against granted patent. Reasons for invalidation are enumerated restrictively: they are pertinent to industrial applicability, order of public, novelty, enlarged concept of novelty, inventive step, detail description, derivation, amendment of new matter addition, first to file, etc.[322]

321. PA Art. 132-3.
322. PA Art. 133.

3. Trial to Confirm the Scope of Right[323]

264. Patent right holder may request the trial to confirm that a certain work of invention by third party is within the scope of his/her right constituting infringement. The third party may also initiate trial to request decision that his/her use is out of patent's scope.

4. Trial for Correction[324]

265. A patent holder may demand a trial for corrections of specifications or drawings to evade invalidation of his/her patent. The correction is allowable only to narrow a claim; to correct a clerical error; to clarify an ambiguous description. Once the decision of correction is affirmed, the patent is deemed applied as corrected claims at initial application.

B. Appeal to Patent Court

266. Patent Court exercises sole jurisdiction for the appeal to decisions of KIPO tribunal. Each panel bodies consist of three to four full-time judges and there is no 'technical judge' in Korean Patent Court. Instead, in-house counsels of various fields of technology conduct counselling for judges to understand substance of arts in every patent case. As with civil litigation, the principles of oral proceedings, burden of pleading and proof apply to patent court proceedings too. The parties may argue fact finding of tribunal and submit new argument or evidence in procedure of Patent Court. Once Patent Court disagrees with the decision of tribunal, it reverses decision and remands the case to trial board. Though Patent Court's decision binds tribunal, tribunal is free from such effect where new assertion or evidence is submitted in trial after reversal. Supreme Court is the court of final appeal against Patent Court's decision.

C. Effects of Confirmed Trial Decision

267. If there is no appeal to Patent Court for first instance trial decision, no final appeal for Patent Courts appellate decision, or Final decision by Supreme Court is rendered, the trial decision shall be confirmed. Confirmed trial decision has final and conclusive effect, and is neither extinct nor altered but for exceptional case of statutory retrial.[325] Furthermore, confirmed trial may not be re-tried by anyone (including third party) as long as it is based on same ground and same evidence.[326] Patent Act provides this rule to protect patentee from repeated trial, and keep his/her legal

323. PA Art. 135.
324. PA Art. 136.
325. PA Art. 178.
326. PA Art. 136.

stability. Meanwhile, the third party may bring up a new trial as long as it is based upon different ground or different evidence with confirmed trial.

D. Relation between Invalidation Trial and Infringement Suit

268. In one hand, the infringer may bring up invalidation trial against plaintiff's patent, which has in rem effect once confirmed. On the other hand, the infringer may assert the invalidity of plaintiff's patent as a defence in infringement litigation. Given such defence is successful, it has no in rem effect to make such patent invalid but the effect to free defendant from liability in such suit. Once the defendant brought up invalidation trial separately, the judge of parallel infringement suit often holds the process to refer to the decision of KIPO tribunal or Patent Court. However, this is judge's discretion and in many cases, the judges of civil suit independently decide the validity of pertinent patent as previous question. Such is more often the case in provisional disposition where promptness is highly demanded.

Chapter 3. Utility Models

§1. Sources: Legislation

269. For small inventions, Utility Model Act provides protections. From long ago, Korea has had Utility Model Act separate from Patent Act. Utility Model Act has been amended thirty times from its initial enactment in 31 December 1961 to 31 January 2014. One thing noteworthy is Utility Model Act has maintained 'grant without examination' rule for a time. Currently, for utility model registration, it is principle to be examined of requirements such as novelty, inventive step, detail description, etc. Meanwhile, Utility Model Act of 1998 has adopted 'grant without examination' system, under which utility model right is granted only after formality review. This was to resolve backlog of examination and to help inventors of small utility devices to obtain right promptly. On the other hand, to cover possible demerits of the system, the right holder was mandated to pass examination before he/she 'exercises' the granted right. In addition, the post grant review was assured, letting any third party to request examination for granted utility model. However, said 'grant without examination' system was abolished through Utility Model Act amendment of 2006 and 'examination before grant' revived to subsists until now.

§2. The Protection of Utility Models

I. Subject Matter

270. The subject matter of Utility Model Act is 'devices'. 'Device' refers to the creation of technical ideas applying the law of nature.[327] In practical term, 'device' here implies 'small inventions of manufacture'. Meanwhile, the Patent Act stipulates 'invention' as 'highly advanced' creation of technical idea utilizing the law of nature. As this, whether the invention is highly advanced is watershed point to discern utility model from invention. However, this criterion is deemed hollow and substituted by the matter of inventive step in practice. Rather, the most critical difference between utility model and invention is that the former comprises only product (device), while the latter comprises product and process. Article 4(1) of Utility Model Act provides, 'A utility model may be granted for a device related to a shape or a structure of an article, or a combination of articles industrially practicable.' excluding process from its subject matter. Other than this difference, utility model and invention are not strictly distinguished in practice. For an instance, any applicant of utility model may alter his/her application into patent during examination process and *vice versa.*[328]

327. Utility Model Act, Art. 2.1.
328. Utility Model Act, Art. 10; PA Art. 53.

II. Patent Act Applied Mutatis Mutandis

271. Utility Model Act applies Patent Act *mutatis mutandis* in many provisions.[329] This is natural considering the intimacy between two Acts, and that Utility Model Act has been taking 'uniformity with Patent Act' as its motto since its amendment of 2006.

III. Difference between Utility Model and Patent

272. The apparent difference between two Acts shall be summarized in the table below. For the other issues, referring to explanations in Patent Act may suffice.

A. Subject Matter

Patent	Highly advanced creation of technical idea utilizing law of nature
Utility Model	Creation of technical idea utilizing law of nature for device related to a shape or a structure of an article, or a combination of articles industrially practicable

B. Inventive Step

Patent	No inventive step for the invention which skilled person in the art may create 'easily' referring to prior arts.
Utility Model	No inventive step for the invention which skilled person in the art may create 'very easily' referring to prior arts

It is easier to obtain utility model right for a small invention than patent, as the standard of inventive step is more lenient.

329. Utility Model Act, Arts 3, 11, 15, 20, 22-6, 28, 30, 33, 41, 44, etc.

C. Duration

Patent	Twenty years as from filing date[330]
Utility Model	Ten years as from filing date[331]

D. Definition of Working

Patent	(1) In cases of a product invention, acts of manufacturing, using, assigning, leasing, importing, or offering for assigning or leasing the product; (2) In cases of a process invention, acts of using the process; (3) In cases of a process invention to manufacture a product, acts of using, assigning, leasing, importing, or offering for assigning or leasing the product manufactured by the process, in addition to the acts mentioned in item (2).
Utility Model	Act of manufacturing, using, assigning, leasing, importing, or offering for assigning or leasing (including displaying for the purpose of assignment or lease) an article to which a device has been applied.[332]

As a process is not the subject matter of Utility Mode, the types of working relevant with process are excluded.

E. Request of Examination

Patent	By anyone within five years as from filing date[333]
Utility Model	By anyone within three years as from filing date[334]

330. PA Art. 88(1).
331. Utility Model Act, Art. 22(1).
332. Utility Model Act, Art. 2. 3.
333. PA Art. 59.
334. Utility Model Act, Art. 12(3).

Chapter 4. Trademarks

§1. SOURCES: LEGISLATION

273. Main source of law for trademark in Korea is Trademark Act. Trademark Act has been amended thirty- seven times since initial enactment of 28 November 1949. Current Act is enforced as of 11 June 2014. Korea has joined four trademark related treaties:

(1) Nice Agreement Concerning the International Classification of Goods and Services for the Purposes of the Registration of Marks (date of enforcement: 8 January 1999).
(2) Trademark Law Treaty (date of enforcement: 25 February 2003).
(3) Protocol Relating to the Madrid Agreement Concerning the International Registration of Marks (date of enforcement: 10 April 2003).
(4) Vienna Agreement Establishing an International Classification of the Figurative Elements of Marks (date of enforcement: 17 April 2011).

Along with Trademark Act, Unfair Competition Prevention and Trade Secret Protection Act (hereinafter, referred as 'Unfair Competition Act') protects well-known business identity in the market. Unfair Competition Act covers broader subject matters than Trademark Act: any type of business identity domestically well known.[335] Unfair Competition Act regards Trademark Act as a special rule, stipulating, 'If any provision of Trademark Act is inconsistent with the provisions of Unfair Competition Act, such provisions of Trademark Act shall preferentially apply.'[336]

§2. SUBJECT MATTER OF PROTECTION

I. Trademark and Service Mark

274. TA Article 2(1) 1. Stipulates:

> 'Trademark' means any of the following items that is used by a person who produces, processes, or sells goods as a business, in order to distinguish the goods from those of others.
>
> (1) Any sign, letter, figure, three-dimensional shape, or the combination thereof;
> (2) Any colour that is not combined with others, the combination of colours, any hologram, movement, or other item that can be visually recognized;
> (3) Any invisible item such as sound, odour, etc., that are expressed by any visual medium such as sign, letter, figure, etc.

335. Trademark and service mark are subcategories of business identity.
336. Unfair Competition Act, Art. 15(1).

TA Article 2(1) 2. Stipulates:

> 'Service mark' means a mark which is used by a person who carries on service business for the purpose of distinguishing his/her service business from those of others.

The provisions for trademark shall be applied *mutatis mutandis* to service mark.[337]

II. Other Marks

275. Marks described below are statutory marks on which trademark protections are conferred and provisions for trademark shall be applied *mutatis mutandis.*

A. *Collective Mark*

276. 'Collective Mark' means a mark which is intended to be used:

(1) by a corporation jointly founded by the persons who produce, manufacture, process, or sell goods as a business or,
(2) by an individual member of said corporation.[338]

B. *Geographical Collective Mark*

277. 'Geographical Indication' means an indication which identifies geographical location of production, manufacture or process of goods when a certain quality, reputation, or characteristic of the goods is essentially attributed to said location.[339]

278. 'Geographical Collective Mark' means a collective mark which is intended to be used:

(1) by a corporation composed solely of the persons who produce, manufacture, or process goods eligible for geographical indication as a business or,
(2) by an individual member of said corporation.[340]

C. *Business Emblem*

279. 'Business emblem' means a mark which is used for the purpose of indicating his/her business by a person who carries on non-profit business.[341]

---

337. TA Art. 2(3).
338. TA Art. 2(1) 3.
339. TA Art. 2(1) 3-2.
340. TA Art. 2(1) 3-4.
341. TA Art. 2(1) 5.

D. Certification Mark

280. 'Certification Mark' means a mark which is intended to be used by a person who carries on the business of certifying the quality, origin, mode of production, or other characteristics of goods or service.[342]

III. Special Types of Symbols Eligible as Trademarks

281. As Trademark Act qualifies any kind of symbol to indicate the source of goods or services as trademark, the sound, odour, colour, etc., are also eligible as trademark as it is. To be noted, these symbols shall be expressed in visually perceivable format to be registered. For instance, the colour shall be expressed in chromaticity; the sound shall be expressed in sonogram or score; the odour shall be described in format of chemical formula or by exemplifying things that gives such fragrances. In many cases, specific colour or odour itself has no distinctiveness by itself. Such colour or odour may obtain registrability as trademark once it obtained distinctiveness through continuous use as a mark.

IV. Trademark and Designated Goods

282. Trademark shall be applied for and registered in connection with designated goods of certain categories. The applicant shall designate one or more categories of goods among the classes provided in Trademark Act Enforcement Rule Article 6. The rule indicates thirty-four classes of goods (from No. 1 through No. 34) and eleven classes of services (from No. 35 through No. 45). As a Member State, Korea follows international goods classification of NICE agreement. Designated goods are always considered with mark in deciding distinctiveness, source confusion, and pertinent use of the mark.

V. Registration

283. The person who is to obtain trademark shall apply for registration at KIPO with the mark and its designated goods. Once application is filed the KIPO officer examines if applied trademark is eligible for registration. The major requirements of eligibility are that the mark is distinctive enough to indicate source of certain goods and has no cause of rejection enumerated in TA Article 7. If multiple parties file for registration on identical or similar mark and goods, the prior applicant has priority (First to file: Article 8). Once a trademark passes the examination and is registered, the trademark right is vested.[343] The registration requirement in Trademark

342. TA Art. 2(1) 4.
343. TA Art. 41(1).

Act is distinguished from Unfair Competition Act, under which any business identity well known in domestic area is eligible for protection regardless of registration. All the explanations above are applicable to service mark too.[344]

§3. Conditions of Protection

I. Distinctiveness

284. In light of trademark's original function as source indication, a trademark must have certain degree of symbolistic power to distinct its goods from others. The trademark without such distinctiveness is rejected[345] and is to be invalidated after registration.[346]

A. *Marks without Distinctiveness*[347]

1. Generic Term (TA Article 6(1) 1.)

285. A trademark consisting solely of a mark indicating the ordinary name of the goods in a common way cannot be registered.[348]

2. A Trademark Used Customarily on the Goods (TA Article 6(1) 2.)

286. Not being a generic term, where the mark is regarded as customary indication of pertinent goods among people concerned with its dealing, such mark has no distinctiveness.[349]

3. Descriptive Mark (TA Article 6(1) 3.)

287. A trademark consisting solely of a mark indicating the origin, quality, raw materials, efficacy, use, quantity, shape (including shapes of packages), price, producing method, processing method, using method or time of the goods is 'descriptive mark'. The reason to exclude these marks from eligibility is that: (1) straightforward descriptions of goods have little distinctiveness, and (2) such marks shall be in public domain so that anybody may use to describe the character of goods. On the other hand, 'suggestive' mark, which implies rather than describes the character of goods, is not deemed descriptive.

---

344. TA Art. 2(3).
345. TA Art. 23(1).
346. TA Art. 71(1) 1.
347. TA Art. 6(1).
348. 'Vaseline' is a generic term: SCt. 1996. 5. 14 – 95 Hoo 1463.
349. 'Napoleon' for cognac is customarily used mark on those goods: SCt. 1985. 1. 22. – 83 Hoo 14.

4. Geographical Name (TA Article 6(1) 4.)

288. A trademark consisting solely of a conspicuous geographical name, the abbreviation thereof or a map is deemed not distinctive.[350] Conspicuous geographical name itself causes ineligibility, even without consumer's misconception as source of relevant goods.

5. Popular Name (TA Article 6 (1) 5.)

289. A trademark consisting solely of a mark indicating a common surname or name in common way cannot be registered. Common name of natural person, corporation, business name, etc., are subject to this provision.[351]

6. A Trademark Consisting Solely of a Simple and Ordinary Mark (TA Article 6(1) 6.)

290. Very short list of alphabets, very common figures, or combinations thereof are deemed not distinctive.[352]

7. The Other Marks of Little Distinctiveness (TA Article 6(1) 7.)

291. A trademark, other than those referred above, which does not enable consumers to recognize the origin of goods is not distinctive. This is a 'catch-all clause' to exclude marks of little distinctiveness. Very simple slogan, mundane expression or symbol to promote sales falls on this ineligibility.[353]

B. Acquisition of Distinctiveness Through Continuous Use

292. The marks lack of distinctiveness may obtain eligibility once it obtained distinctiveness through continuous use. Trademark Act allows such eligibility for descriptive mark, geographical name, popular name, and simple and ordinary marks.[354] Though Trademark Act excludes 'the other marks of little distinctiveness' from eligibility, Supreme Court articulates such type of mark may also be registered once it obtained distinctiveness through continuous use.[355]

---

350. 'Georgia' is a conspicuous geographical name: SCt. 2012. 12. 13 – 2011 Hoo 958.
351. 'Lee' is a common surname: SCt. 1989. 12. 22 – 89 Hoo 582.
352. 'V2' (SCt. 2001. 7. 24 – 2000 Hoo 3906); 'K-Y' (SCt. 1999. 8. 24 – 99 Hoo 1461); ' ' (Sct. 2007. 3. 16. -2006 Hoo 3632).
353. 'Believe it or not' for museum business: SCt. 1994. 11. 18 – 94 Hoo 173.
354. TA Art. 6(2).
355. SCt 2006. 5. 12 – 2005 Hoo 339; SCt 2003. 7. 11 – 2001 Hoo 2863.

C. *Loss of Distinctiveness Through Continuous Use*

293. In contrast with acquisition of distinctiveness through continuous use, some initially distinctive marks lose their distinctiveness as they are widely used in public, being a generic term. 'Aspirin',[356] 'Jeep'[357] are examples of such cases in Korea.

II. Other Causes to Reject Registration

A. *Marks Identical or Similar with National or International Emblems*

294.

(1) Trademarks which are identical or similar to the national flag, the national emblem, colours, medals, decorations or badges of Korea, or seals or signs used for indicating supervision or certification by Korea or public institutions.
(2) Trademarks which are identical or similar to the national flags of allied nations of the Paris Convention for the Protection of Industrial Property, member nations of the World Trade Organization, or contracting parties to the Trademark Law Treaty (hereafter referred to as 'allied nations, etc.').
(3) Trademarks which are identical or similar to the titles, abbreviated names or marks of the Red Cross, the International Olympic Committee, or renowned international organizations.
(4) Trademarks identical or similar:
    (a) To armorial bearings, flags, medals, decorations, or badges of allied nations, etc. which are designated by the Commissioner of KIPO under Paris Convention.
    (b) To titles, abbreviated names, armorial bearings, flags, medals, decorations, or badges of inter-governmental international organizations in which allied nations, etc., join.
(5) Trademarks 'the symbol' and 'designated goods' of which are identical or similar to:
    (a) Supervision or certification seals or signs of allied nations, etc., or their public organizations.
    (b) The goods where said seals or signs are used.

B. *Disparaging Marks Etc. (TA Article 7(1) 2.)*

295. Trademarks which:

(1) Falsely indicate a connection with a State, race, ethnic group, public organization, religion, or famous deceased person.

---

356. SCt. 1977. 5. 10 – 76 Da 1721.
357. SCt. 1992. 11. 10 – 92 Hoo 414.

(2) Criticize, insult or are liable to defame them.

Supreme Court decided, 'Darkie' as a mark possibly defames a race.[358] 'Mozart' is a name of famous deceased person, but if the mark contains no indication of 'false connection' between that name and goods, this rule shall not be applied.[359]

C. *Mark Similar to the Symbol of Non-profit Public Entity (TA Article 7(1) 3.)*

296. This clause applies to trademarks which are identical or similar to famous marks indicating non-profit business of the State, a public organization, its agencies, public corporations, or indicating non-profit public services.

D. *Mark against Public Order (TA Article 7(1) 4.)*

297. Where the content of trademark itself is against virtuous customs or public order or, where the use of trademark causes harm to virtuous customs or public order. The marks of obscene designs or curse fall on this provision. In practice however, this provision is applied more often for where the 'use' of a certain mark causes harm to public order. Supreme Court has interpreted this situation quite leniently. For example, occupying a Korean term 'Woo-Ri (means "our")' as a trademark of banking service was blocked by this provision. Supreme Court articulated:

> If a party occupies such a word as trademark and exclude others from using 'Woo-Ri', many competitors will be deprived of fair pronominal expression to indicate their banking services in various situations. It is where a use of trademark harms public order.[360]

E. *Mark Similar with Emblem of Authorized Exhibition (TA Article 7(1) 5.)*

298. Trademark which is identical or similar to, a medal, certificate of merit or decoration awarded at an exhibition held by or with approval by the government of Korea or at an exhibition held by or with approval by the government of a foreign country.

F. *Marks Mainly Consist of Well-Known Name of Others (TA Article 7(1) 6.)*

299. Trademarks containing the name, title or trade name, portrait, signature or seal, pseudonym, professional name or pen name of well-known other persons, or

358. SCt. 1987. 3. 24. – 86 Hoo 163.
359. SCt. 1998. 2. 13. – 97 Hoo 938.
360. SCt. 2009. 5. 28 – 2007 Hoo 3301.

an abbreviation thereof: Provided, that this shall not apply where the consent of the person concerned has been obtained.[361] This clause is to protect the personality of individual, rather than source indication power. Hence, no one may exploit other's fame for commercial interest without consent. Supreme Court interprets the 'person' here refers to person 'alive' only.[362]

G. *Marks Confusingly Similar with Other's Mark (TA Article 7(1) 7, 9, 10.)*

300. Trademark Act treats mark identical or similar with others ineligible due to its possibility of confusion with other's mark. The possibility to cause confusion is tied to famousness of the mark. If the mark referred is not famous, only the mark highly similar with it causes confusion. On the contrary, if the mark referred is famous enough, even slight similarity may cause confusion. The famousness of marks referred increase gradually from TA Article 7(1) 7.–9., 10.

1. Mark Identical or Similar with Other's Mark Applied and Registered Priorly (TA Article 7(1) 7.)

301. (1) If X applied for a trademark prior to Y and, (2) Y applied for trademark registration for same or similar mark on same or similar goods with those of X, and (3) X obtained trademark registration eventually,[363] X's application shall be rejected by this clause, which represents the 'first to file' doctrine of Korean Trademark Act.

2. Mark Identical or Similar with 'Well-Known' Mark of Others (TA Article 7(1) 9.)

302. The trademark is unregistrable if: (1) It is identical with or similar to another person's trademark which is well-known among consumers, and (2) Its designated goods are identical with or similar to those of well-known mark. The well-known mark here may be either registered or non-registered mark. This is an exceptional rule of first to file doctrine, as even unregistered mark prevents subsequent registration of junior mark, which may cause confusion.

3. Mark Possibly Causes Confusion with 'Very Well-Known' Mark of Others or Harm Distinctiveness (TA Article 7(1) 10.)

303. Trademark possibly to cause confusion with goods or business of another person or to harm the distinctiveness or fame of another person's mark is

361. SCt. 2013. 10. 31 – 2012 Hoo 1033: '2NE1' is a name of well-known female singers group in Korea. Defendant is ineligible to register '2NE1' as trademark without consent of said group.
362. SCt. 1998. 2. 13. – 97 Hoo 938.
363. Registration of X's trademark may occur either before or after Y's application date.

unregistrable.[364] Regardless of the stipulation, prior mark protected by this provision is limited to 'very well-known' mark.[365] Consequently, the standard to recognize similarity between marks or goods for confusion is relatively relaxed in this clause. Identity of 'motif' in marks suffices.[366] Where the designated goods are different, the gap is bridged if customers possibly believe that the goods are from same sources or under a certain sponsorship.[367] Very recently, TA was amended to adopt the unregistrability of a mark that may harm distinctiveness or fame of well-known mark of other's.

H. Deceptive Mark (TA Article 7(1) 11.)

304. Trademarks which are liable to mislead or deceive consumers as to the quality of the goods are unregistrable.[368]

1. Deception of Quality

305. 'Deception of quality' is widely recognized in various cases. Any trademark possibly misleads the geographical source,[369] characteristics of goods,[370] class of goods the mark represents,[371] is estimated as mark of quality deception.

2. Misleading Customers

306. Supreme Court has stipulated that using 'similar mark' to 'similar goods' may fall on this clause. Misleading by such marks is quite leniently recognized. Thus, if X uses similar mark of Y while Y's mark is known among customers as 'particular person's belonging' (it needs not be well-known or known as Y's mark), it triggers application of this clause. Further, if the goods of X and Y are in 'economic relevance' (they need not belong to same or similar classification, only probability of same source may suffice), the application of this clause is completed.[372]

I. Mark Filed under Unfair Purpose (TA Article 7(1) 12.)

307. Trademark identical or similar to any trademark, which is recognized as indicating the goods of a particular person by customers in the inside or outside of

364. TA Art. 7(1) 10.
365. SCt. 2004. 4. 27. – 2002 Hoo 1850, etc.
366. SCt. 1995. 10. 12 – 95 Hoo 576.
367. SCt. 2007. 12 27 – 2006 Hoo 664.
368. TA Art. 7(1) 11.
369. SCt. 1994. 12. 9. – 94 Hoo 623.
370. SCt. 2000. 10. 13. – 99 Hoo 628.
371. SCt. 2004. 5. 13 – 2002 Hoo 2006.
372. SCt. 2010. 1. 28 – 2009 Hoo 3268; SCt. 2004. 3. 11 – 2001 Hoo 3187.

Korea, and which are used for unjust purposes, such as obtaining unjust profits or inflicting harm on the particular person, is unregistrable.[373] This provision mainly prevents the unfair act to intercept 'known to customers but unregistered' mark of others, to request purchase or cause detriment. The required famousness of intercepted trademark is similar with that of TA Article 7(1) 11. (known among customers as 'particular person's belonging'). The said unfair purpose of trademark applicant may be assumed by circumstantial facts such as, famousness of intercepted mark, similarity between two marks, economic relevance of goods, history of dispute, etc.

J. *Functional Marks (TA Article 7(1) 13.)*

308. Trademark consisting solely of three-dimensional shapes, colours, the combination of colours, sound or odour essential to secure the functions of goods or their packaging is unregistrable.[374] Trademark excludes the functional trademark mainly related to function or shape of goods other than source indication. Such shall be protected by design or patent.

K. *Geographical Origin of Wine and Spirits (TA Article 7(1) 14.)*

309. Trademark that indicates geographical origin of wines or spirits in a member nation of the World Trade Organization for such goods or similar goods is unregistrable, unless, the person entitled to use the geographical indications applies for geographical collective mark on such goods.[375]

§4. Formalities (Procedure for Obtaining Protection, Establishing and Maintaining Trademarks)

I. Application

A. *In General*

310. Applicant shall file for registration of trademark at KIPO. Each trademark shall specifically designate one or more classes of goods. Each application shall be made on individual marks and application of multiple marks in one document is not allowed.[376] Trademark is established as of registration. The applicant or trademark right holder who wants to enlarge the classes of designated goods may apply for addition of designated goods.

373. TA Art. 7(1) 12.
374. TA Art. 7(1) 13.
375. TA Art. 7(1) 14.
376. TA Art. 10.

B. First to File

311.

(1) If multiple applications are filed on different days for the same or similar trademark on the same or similar goods, only one person who files an application earlier than the others shall be entitled to trademark registration.[377]
(2) If multiple applications are filed on the same day for the same or similar trademark on the same or similar goods, only one applicant designated by agreement among applicants shall be entitled to trademark registration. If they fail to reach any agreement, or they are unable to do so, only one applicant determined by lot drawn by the Commissioner of KIPO shall be entitled to have the trademark registered.[378]

II. Examination and Public Review

312. Examiner of KIPO is in charge of examination. Examiner shall reject on the grounds of unregistrablilty described above. Before final rejection, the notice of ground for rejection shall precede, assuring pertinent chance of reaction for applicant.[379] The applicant who disagrees with rejection may appeal to trial board of KIPO with thirty days as from the date he/she received the notice of final rejection. Examiner shall publish the application by gazette to notice to public. Anyone may file objection with documents describing the ground and pertinent evidence. Such objection shall be made within two months as from publication date.[380] The objection of reasonable ground shall lead examiner to final rejection against application of trademark registration.

III. Registration

313. The examiner who failed to locate any ground of rejection shall decide trademark registration.[381] The applicant, who received notice of approval, shall pay registration fee and the Commissioner of KIPO registers trademark.[382]

§5. Ownership and Transfer (Assignment: Licenses)

I. The Establishment and Transfer of Trademark

314. Trademark right begins to exist as from registration.[383] Trademark right is transferrable and any trademark right may be divided by designated goods so as to

377. TA Art. 8(1).
378. TA Art. 8(2).
379. TA Art. 23(2).
380. TA Art. 25.
381. TA Art. 30.
382. TA Art. 39.
383. TA Art. 41.

be transferred. In such cases, similar designated goods shall be transferred all together.[384] The assignment and establishment of pledge shall be registered to take effect.[385] Where the trademark right is jointly owned, no joint owner may transfer his/her share or establish a pledge on the share without obtaining the consent of all the other joint owners.[386] The rights of business mark, collective mark and certification mark are not transferrable in principle.[387]

II. License

315. Trademark right owner may establish exclusive or non-exclusive license to another person. Where trademark right is joint-owned, unanimous consent of joint owners are necessary for establishing license.[388] Establishment of exclusive and non-exclusive license takes effect without registration, whereas registration is required to take third party effect for such licenses.[389] After registration, the licensee can claim priority against the holder of right, which is incompatible with such license. Any type of licensee shall obtain permission of licensor to transfer, establish a pledge or sub-license his/her right to a third party.[390] As with Patent Act, Trademark Act confers equivalent power on exclusive licensee for remedies against infringement.

§6. Scope of Exclusive Rights

316. In trademark, the distinction between right to use and right to exclude plays critical role. Trademark Act articulates 'The trademark right holder has exclusive right to use registered mark on its designated goods.'[391] Consequently, right holder's privilege to use or give a license is defined to 'identical' mark on 'identical' designated goods, and does not extend to realm of 'similarity'. Rather, if the right holder uses his/her mark or gives license in the range of similarity, causing confusion with other's business, the right holder shall lose trademark.[392] If the registered trade mark is not used in identical manner for a certain period, the registration shall be cancelled; the use of similar mark cannot prevent such cancellation.[393] On the other side, once a mark is registered, the third party's acts to use similar mark on same or similar goods are deemed infringement,[394] and trademark holder is entitled

384. TA Art. 54(1).
385. TA Art. 56.
386. TA Art. 54(5).
387. TA Art. 54(7), (9), (10).
388. TA Art. 54(6).
389. TA Art. 58.
390. TA Art. 55(5), (6); TA Art. 57(3), (4).
391. TA Art. 50.
392. TA Art. 73(1) 2.
393. TA Art. 73(1) 3.
394. TA Art. 66(1).

of remedies against such infringements. To sum up, the right to use 'similar mark' with registered trademark belongs neither to right holder nor to a third party.

§7. Limitations of the Scope of Trademark Protection

I. Statutory Limitations of Trademark Right

317. If the use of trademark conforms to any of following, the user is free from infringement allegation. This provision works as enumeration of 'fair use' in trademark law.

A. Trademark Same with User's Name

318. Any person may use other's mark provided that it is mere use of his/her name, trade name, portrait, signature, seal or well-known pseudonym, stage name, pen name, and well-known abbreviation thereof, in common ways.[395] If the name is of well-known person, the trademark rather bears cause of invalidation under TA Article 7(1) 6. Thus, this provision is applicable where a name of ordinary person is preoccupied by a third party and the owner of such name uses it as source indication of his/her goods. On the other side, if the owner of name uses the mark in way of unfair competition after the trademark is established, it constitutes trademark infringement.[396]

B. Descriptive Use

319. If one uses trademark indicating denomination, place of origin, quality, raw materials, efficacy, use, quantity, shape, price, producing method, processing method, using method, etc., of goods in a common way, it does not constitute infringement even though such indication is same or similar with registered trademark of others.[397] The generic term or merely descriptive mark has no distinctiveness, and is invalid under TA Article 6(1) 3. Trademark Act regards use of such mark as lawful even before the mark is officially invalidated, allowing defence for third party against infringement allegation.

C. Name Customarily Used for Goods/Conspicuously Geographical Name

320. If one uses name which is conspicuously geographical or customarily used for such goods, it is not infringement regardless that such geographical name or

395. TA Art. 51(1) 1.
396. TA Art. 51(3).
397. TA Art. 51(1) 2.

customary name is already registered as trademark by other person.[398] Such marks are invalid under TA Article 6(1) 2., 4. for lack of distinctiveness. Trademark Act regards use of such mark as lawful even before the mark is officially invalidated, allowing defence for third party against infringement allegation.

D. *Functional Mark*

321. If a registered trademark consists of shapes, colours, the combination of colours, sound or odour essential to secure the functions of the designated goods of a registered trademark or their packaging, use of such mark does not constitute infringement.[399] Such functional mark is invalid under TA Article 7(1) 13. Trademark Act regards use of such mark as lawful even before the mark is officially invalidated, allowing defence for third party against infringement allegation.

II. Abuse of Trademark Right

322. Supreme Court acknowledges two types as abuse of trademark right:

(1) Exercising trademark right to pursue unjust profit, harming fair trade or competition rule.
(2) Exercising trademark whose invalidity is clear.

Any type of above shall function as effective defence in trade mark infringement action.

A. *Type of Unfair Competition Purpose*

323. Where the trademark right owner registers the mark or exercises the right to free ride other's business renown in the market, other than to identify his/her goods, such is deemed abuse of right, leading to failure of execution.[400] Where the purpose of exercise is to scrounge unjust profit from defendant, it is also deemed abuse of right. Supreme Court determined:

> The plaintiff was former business partner of defendant over pertinent goods (bottled beer in this case). After the business was terminated, plaintiff took a notice that the defendant had not registered trademark for the goods by then, and preoccupied the trademark through registration. Subsequently, plaintiff threatened defendant with injunction as a right holder and demanded to reopen the business with him. Upon these facts, plaintiff's exercise of trademark right is estimated unfair enough to harm fair and free trade rules. Thus, defendant's

398. TA Art. 51(1) 3.
399. TA Art. 51(1) 4.
400. SCt. 2007. 1. 25 – 2005 Da 67223.

argument that such trademark right exercise shall be incapacitated has its ground.[401]

B. Type of Clear Invalidity

324. Supreme Court has taken the position that the trademark right shall be upheld so long as its registration subsists, and anyone that would contest its validity shall take track of invalidation trial other than arguing validity of plaintiff's mark as defence in infringement action. However, Supreme Court recently changed its attitude about this issue through en banc decision promulgating, 'given the invalidity of registered trademark is clear, the exercise of such defected right shall be abuse of right and defendant may invoke it as defence, regardless of the cause of invalidity.'[402]

III. Prior User's Right

325. Where a person had been using the mark before the same or similar mark was registered, the prior user may use the mark continuously under certain conditions. This is an exceptional rule of first to file regime of Korean Trademark Act. To be entitled to prior user's right, the prior use shall:

(1) have been started before the filing date of registered mark without purpose of unfair competition, and (2) have led certain amount of source indication power among domestic consumers in relevant market.[403]

Meanwhile, the trademark holder may request pertinent measure to prior user to prevent consumer's confusion in case that such right is established.[404] Further, Trademark Act confers protection by lenient requirement on prior user who had been using his/her name or trade name as trade mark. For those users, the requirement of (2) is exempted.[405]

IV. Limitation from Copyright, Design Right of Others

326. Where the use of trademark conflicts with copyright or design right of others which was filed prior to registered trademark's filing date, trademark right holder may not use his/her trademark without consent of such copyright holder or design right holder.[406] Subsequently, the trademark right holder cannot exercise his/

401. SCt. 2006. 2. 24 – 2004 Ma 101.
402. SCt. 2012. 10. 18 – 2010 Da 103000.
403. TA Art. 57-3 (1).
404. TA Art 57-3 (3).
405. TA Art. 57-3 (2).
406. TA Art. 53.

her right against such copyright holder or design right holder. However, the exercise of trademark right against third party other than such right holders is not influenced by said rule, and the third party may not invoke said rule as defence against trademark infringement allegation.[407]

V. Exhaustion

327. As with other intellectual property rights, trademark right is also subject to exhaustion. Thus, the right holder may not claim trademark right against subsequent use once the trademark goods are lawfully purchased. Nevertheless, the rule does not apply to excessive repair, which is a 'reproduction' of goods. Supreme Court determined that selling disposed 'one time use' cameras after renovation constitutes trademark infringement, if original trademarks are on such recycled cameras.[408] In international view, exhaustion is in respect to whether parallel importation constitutes trademark infringement. Common view and Supreme Court regard parallel import legitimate as the trademark right is internationally exhausted when it was lawfully sold abroad.[409] Nevertheless, if the quality of imported goods is too poor in comparison with goods sold by retailers in Korea, or licensee separately manufactures pertinent goods in Korea, parallel import is banned to protect lawful interest of said retailers or licensees in Korea.[410]

§8. Use Requirements

I. Definition of 'Trademark Use' in Trademark Act

328. The concept of trademark use plays critical role in deciding infringement. Besides, it is decisive factor when determining trademark registration is cancelled by 'non-use' or 'improper use'. Trademark Act Article 2(1) 7. stipulates the definition of trademark use as either:

(1) Indicating a trademark on goods or packages of goods.
(2) Transferring or delivering goods or packages of goods on which a trademark is indicated, or displaying, exporting or importing them for such purpose.
(3) Indicating a trademark on advertisement, on goods, price lists, transaction documents, signboards, or tags and displaying or distributing it.

With regard to service mark use, the definition of trademark use shall be applied *mutatis mutandis*.[411] However, considering the difference of where and how service

407. SCt. 2006. 9. 11 – 2006 Ma 232.
408. SCt. 2003. 4. 11 – 2002 Do 3445.
409. SCt. 2002. 9. 24 – 99 Da 42322.
410. SCt. 2005. 6. 9 – 2002 Da 61965; SCt. 2006. 10. 13 – 2006 Da 40423; SCt. 2010. 5. 17 – 2010 Do 790.
411. TA Art. 2(3).

mark is used in practice, the simple *mutatis mutandis* application is sometimes unsuitable. Consequently, the amendment of definition clause of trademark use is under design in order to reflect individuality of service mark use appropriately.

II. Non-use of Trademark

329. While conforming to definition of trademark use, it is not trademark use unless it works as 'source indication'. Supreme Court applies this norm where the trademark is used only for design purpose,[412] introduction, or illustration of goods and its utility.[413] It is the same where the trademark is used for comparison advertisement, consumer's campaign, or parodies.

III. Trademark Use in Domain Name or Searching Keywords

330. In internet circumstance, 'domain squatting' and 'keyword stuffing' often matter in light of trademark use. With regard to domain squatting, it is mattered whether the act to preoccupy domain name containing other's trademark and to lead customers to squatter's site conforms to trademark use. In keyword stuffing, third party buys keyword consists of other's trademark from ISP, and uses it to lure consumers. The lure often happens automatically by meta-tag encryption as well as misleading web crawlers by showing lurer's page as relevant search result. Supreme Court categorizes trademark use in domain name or searching keywords into two types: (1) to utilize other's trademark only as a measure to expose his/her goods to consumers, not as a measure to confuse source of goods ultimately; and (2) to utilize other's trademark in the way to confuse its source. The trademark infringement is recognized only for the latter type.[414]

331. Supreme Court case of 2004. 5. 14 – 2002 Da 13782 typically illustrates this norm. In this case, defendant occupied domain name of 'www.viagra.co.kr' prior to Pfizer. Meanwhile, defendant advertised and sold in such web page not 'Viagra' or other similar medicaments, but health foods such as mineral water, arrowroot juice which he manufactured. Moreover, all goods sold bore defendant's trademark of 'Sane Sane' other than 'Viagra' or 'Pfizer'. Supreme Court ruled that defendant's deed to lure internet crawlers who are interested in Viagra by means of using such trademark is not trademark use; because defendant exploited trademark Viagra as a bait, not an ultimate method of consumer confusion in purchase (the consumers knew what they were buying were not the products of Pfizer). Instead, Supreme Court recognized defendant's deed as 'dilution of integrity to very well-known mark of others', which constitutes violation of Unfair Competition Act.

412. SCt. 2013. 1. 24 – 2011 Da 18802.
413. SCt. 2011. 1. 13 – 2010 Do 5994; SCt. 2005. 6. 10 – 2005 Do 1637.
414. SCt. 2011. 8. 25. – 2010 Do 7088; SCt. 2008. 9. 25. – 2006 Da 51577.

332. If a cybersquatter occupies domain name of other's domestically well-known trademark and forces purchase or prevents use of that domain name, such constitutes violation of Unfair Competition Act.

§9. Duration of Protection: Renewal – Termination

333. Trademark right exists ten years as from registration date, and may be renewed in the unit of ten years upon application.[415] There is no limitation for number of renewals. The right holder shall pay fee for subsistence of trademark right, and if he/she fails to pay such fee, the right shall extinct. Trademark right also extinct upon abandonment.

§10. Infringement and Remedies

I. Infringement

A. Original Type of Infringement

334. As trademark holder has exclusive right to use the registered mark on designated goods, any act of using identical mark on identical goods with registered mark without right holders consent constitutes infringement.

B. Acts Deemed Infringement

335. Additionally, Trademark Act deems following acts infringement, extending the scope of trademark infringement to realm of 'similarity':[416]

(1) Using a mark identical with other's trademark on similar goods.
(2) Using a mark similar to other's trademark on identical goods.
(3) Using a mark similar to other's trademark on similar goods.

Further, Trademark Act also deems following 'preliminary acts' infringement:

(1) Delivering, selling, forging, imitating, or possessing a mark identical with or similar to other's trademark with intention to use, or to have another person use, on any goods identical with or similar to the designated goods.[417]
(2) Manufacturing, delivering, selling, or possessing tools with intention to forge or imitate, or to have a third person forge or imitate, trademark of other's.[418]

415. TA Art. 42.
416. TA Art. 66(1) 1.
417. TA Art. 66(1) 2.
418. TA Art. 66(1) 3.

(3) Keeping, for a purpose of transfer or delivery, goods identical with or similar to the designated goods on which another person's trademark or any other similar trademark is used.[419]

C. *Co-infringement of Trademark Infringement (Indirect Infringement)*

336. Under a general rule of torts, any act to induce or aid direct infringement of trademark give a rise to co-infringement liability, if done in wilfulness or negligence. Recently, a special type of co-infringement of trademark is mattered in internet open market. This is because open market often works as an intermediary for transactions of infringing goods. Supreme Court stipulates that all of the following criteria should be met for co-infringement liability of such intermediaries:[420]

(1) That the illegality of transacted goods on intermediary's open market is objectively clear.
(2) That the manager of such open market is aware of situation by notice of trademark right holder or spontaneously.
(3) That the control and handling against such situation is technically and economically possible.

II. Remedies

337. As Trademark Act confers equivalent power on exclusive licensee for remedies against infringement, the 'trademark right holder' hereinafter refers to 'owner of trademark and exclusive licensee', unless it is articulated as 'owner of trademark'.

A. *Prohibition Order (Injunction)*

338.

(1) Trademark right holder may demand a person who infringes or is likely to infringe the trademark right to discontinue or prevent the infringement.
(2) Where trademark right holder demands prohibition order, he/she may demand the destruction of products by which infringement was committed, the removal of the facilities used for the act of infringement, or other necessary measures.[421]

Further, prohibition may be ordered in form of provisional disposition, which may be rendered with plaintiff's vindication of 'right to be preserved' and 'necessity of preservation' under Part IV. of Civil Execution Act.

419. TA Art. 66(1) 4.
420. SCt. 2012. 12. 4 – 2010 Ma 817.
421. TA Art. 65.

B. Damages

339. Infringement of trademark right is an act of tort. Damages are available to torts of wilfulness or negligence in accordance with relevant provisions in Civil Act.[422] However, in most cases, it is hard for plaintiff to prove causal relation between infringement and actual damages. To alleviate this problem and protect plaintiff effectively, Trademark Act provides several special articles of damage calibration rules, which are based upon some legal presumptions.

1. 'Number of Transferred Articles by Infringer' X 'Right Holder's Profit per Unit'[423]

340. In measuring damages, the amount of losses may be calculated by multiplying 'the number of articles infringer transferred' by 'the right holder's possible profit per unit of the article'. In such cases, the compensation shall be determined between the amount that right holder's total capability of sales would have produced as maximum, and the amount that right holder actually has sold under circumstance of infringement. Where defendant successfully attests the amount that plaintiff would not have obtained even without infringement, such amount shall be deducted from aforesaid damage amount. The burden of proof for such special facts goes to defendant.

2. Presumption of Infringer's Profit to Damages

341. If infringer has gained any profit by infringement, the relevant amount of profit shall be presumed to be the amount of damages sustained by trademark right holder.[424] As with TA Article 67(1), this provision is regarded applicable only where trademark right holder produces or sales goods by himself/herself.[425] Whereas the structure of provision seems more straightforward than TA Article 67(1), it is generally hard for plaintiff to prove 'profit' of defendant.

3. Reasonable Royalty

342. Plaintiff may choose the amount of reasonable royalty as damages against trademark infringement.[426] In contrast with damages of reasonable royalty in patent, Supreme Court requires trademark holder to have used the mark himself/herself for entitlement of reasonable royalty damages.[427] For the damages of TA Article 67(1) or (2), court may exercise its discretion, deducting it if not wilful infringement or of

422. Civil Act, Art. 750.
423. TA Art. 67(1).
424. TA Art. 67(2).
425. SCt. 2009. 10. 29 – 2007 Da 22521.
426. TA Art. 67(3).
427. SCt. 2008. 3. 27 – 2005 Da 75002.

gross negligence.[428] In contrast with that, there is no space of discretion and the reasonable royalty is guaranteed as base amount of damages for every infringement. The 'reasonable royalty' here denotes objective amount of money which would have been paid if infringer had gone into a license contract with trademark right holder. If any case of prior license exists, the actual amount of royalty may be standard; if no such case exists, the practical royalty in the field of work will be criteria.

4. Decision of Damages by Discretion

343. Where it is difficult to decide damages by TA Article 67(1) through (3), court may fix considerable damages on its discretion in the light of total purport and evidence in litigation.[429] This is supplemental rule provided for plaintiff who evidently suffered damages by infringement but eventually failed to prove any of its amounts.

5. Statutory Damages

344. Trademark right holder may claim compensation up to KRW 50 million against infringer who used trademark and its goods identically. In this case, court may decide reasonable amount of damages in discretion within said amount of money.[430]

6. Presumption of Wilfulness

345. Trademark right holders may indicate that the mark is registered when they use it.[431] In that case, the infringer is presumed to know the registration of trademark when infringement occurs.[432]

III. Return of Unjust Enrichment

346. Trademark right holder may seek for return of unjust enrichment caused by infringement selectively with damages. The option of 'return of unjust enrichment' is merited for plaintiff in light of extinctive prescription (long term of ten years, while that of damages is short term of three years). On the other hand, there is no applicability of presumption rules of TA Article 67; plaintiff bears heavy burden of proof for causation between infringement and defendant's enrichment.

---

428. TA Art. 67(4).
429. TA Art. 67(5).
430. TA Art. 67-2(1).
431. TA Art. 90.
432. TA Art. 68.

IV. Recovery of Reputation

347. Upon request of a trademark right holder, court may order the infringer who has injured the business reputation of right holder to take necessary measures to restore business reputation.[433] Typically, the harm of trademark right holder's reputation is caused by low quality of infringing articles. The representative measure to restore business reputation of right holder is to publish the fact of infringement on newspaper, magazine, etc.

V. Criminal Sanctions

348. In Korea, trademark infringements are subject to criminal sanctions. As a representative example, any person who infringes trademark right shall be punished by imprisonment for not more than seven years or by a fine not exceeding KRW 100 million.[434]

§11. Overlapping and Relation to Other Intellectual Property

349. Where a trademark is well-known to public in Korea, the confusing use of such mark triggers application of Unfair Competition Act too. In this aspect, the rule of Trademark Act and Unfair Competition overlaps. Article 15 of Unfair Competition Act stipulates the status of Trademark Act as a special rule of Unfair Competition Act, which shall be applied first where two Acts conflict or compete. Nonetheless, according to the cases, the claim of unfair competition functions as a defence against trademark infringement allegations. For the detail, the relevant explanations in Trademark Act (Abuse of trademark right) shall be referred to.

§12. Tribunals Relevant to Trademark Right

I. Trial against Rejection of Registration[435]

350. The applicant who received final rejection from the examiner may appeal to KIPO tribunal board within thirty days as from the date he/she received the letter of decision.

II. Invalidation Trial[436]

351. Any interested party or examiner may file for invalidation at KIPO tribunal board against registered trademark. The representative cause of invalidation shall be

433. TA Art. 69.
434. TA Art. 93.
435. TA Art. 70-2.
436. TA Art. 71.

lack of distinctiveness (TA Article 6) and unregistrabilities stipulated in TA Article 7. To be noted, marks mainly consist of common name (TA Article 7(1) 6.); marks confusingly similar with other's mark (TA Article 7(1) 7., 8., 9.); and marks against geographical origin for wine and spirit (TA Article 7(1) 14.) are incontestable with validity after five years from the registration date.[437] Once the trial decision of invalidation is confirmed, the mark is deemed unregistered from the first.[438]

III. Trial to Confirm the Scope of Right

352. Trial to Confirm the Scope of Right (TCSR) denotes trial to decide whether certain mark used falls within similarity scope of registered mark and its goods.[439] There are two types of TCSR: (1) positive type of TCSR, where the right holder demands confirmation that defendant's mark and goods fall within similarity scope of plaintiff's; and (2) negative type of TCSR, where the alleged infringer demands confirmation that his/her mark or goods is not similar with that of right holder. The confirmed TCSR decision has no binding effect to courts of subsequent infringement suit.

IV. Trial for Cancellation of Trademark Registration

353. Trademark Act Article 73 enumerates causes of cancellation. In contrast with invalidation, which has retroactive effect, the cancellation nullifies trademark registration to the future. Two representative types of cancellation trial are the followings.

A. Cancellation upon Inappropriate Use

354. Where the owner of a trademark right intentionally arouses consumer's confusion for quality of goods or with business of another person by using the registered mark, any person may file for cancellation trial against such trademark.[440] The confusion here includes confusion of sponsorship as well as confusion of good's source. This clause has nature as a penalty for disturbing soundness of transaction order on the plea of trademark right exercise. Once the trial decision is confirmed, trademark right expires to the future, and the trademark owner shall not apply for registration on the same or similar mark for three years as from such cancellation.[441]

437. TA Art. 76(1).
438. TA Art. 71(3).
439. TA Art. 75.
440. TA Art. 73(1) 2.
441. TA Art. 7(5).

B. Cancellation upon Non-use

355. Where neither trademark right holder nor licensee has used the trademark in Korea for three consecutive years before filing date of cancellation trial, the registration of such trademark shall be cancelled upon request of interested party.[442] The type of trademark use here is same with those enumerated in TA Article 2(1) 7. Namely: (1) indicating a trademark on goods or packages of goods; (2) transferring or delivering goods or packages of goods on which a trademark is indicated, or displaying, exporting, or importing them for such purpose; (3) indicating a trademark on advertisement, on goods, price lists, transaction documents, signboards, or tags and displaying or distributing it.

356. The advertisement on trademark shall be in relation to goods, and the goods shall be in practical commerce or preliminary state of practical commerce. The token use of trademark to avoid cancellation does not suffice such standards.[443] To evade cancellation upon non-use, the identical mark must be used for identical goods with registered ones. To use a similar mark or to use on similar goods is not enough. Trademark owner shall attest that the registered mark has ever been used in Korea within three years before filing date of trial. Once the trial decision is confirmed, trademark right expires to the future, and trademark owner shall not apply for registration on the same or similar mark for three years as from such cancellation.[444]

442. TA Art. 73(1) 3.
443. SCt. 1992. 8. 18 – 92 Hoo 209.
444. TA Art. 7(5).

Chapter 5. Trade Names

§1. Sources: Legislation

357. Korean Commercial Act provides some regulations for trade name in Article 18 through Article 28. Commercial Act grasps the side of trade name as source indicator of business, conferring some protective measures against free riding of others. However, large portion of articles are regulations about eligibility of trade names, liabilities for lending of trade name, effect of non-use for registered trade name, etc. Hence, it is somewhat irrelevant to regard the rules of trade name in Commercial Act mainly as rules of 'intellectual property'. On the other hand, once a trade name is used as a source indicator of business, it triggers application of trademark law or unfair competition law according to its State of registration or recognition to public. In fact, trade name is stipulated as important subject in Trademark Act and Unfair Competition Act. Thus, it may be sufficient to rely on the description of Trademark Act or Unfair Competition Act for trade name as intellectual property. The followings are brief explanations of trade name regulations in Commercial Act.

§2. The Protection of Trade Names

358. A merchant may designate his/her trade name free.[445] Registration of trade name is not obligatory, whereas the company shall register its trade name. The company shall indicate its kind in trade name and no company may use false kind indication in its trade name.[446]

359. Once a trade name is registered, no other merchant may register same trade name for same or similar business in same local area (Special city, Metropolitan city, City, and Province).[447]

360. Where a certain trade name is occupied by a merchant, no other merchant may use trade name that may cause confusion with such business in bad faith.[448] Punishment by fine shall be imposed for violation of this rule.[449] The bad faith here denotes the intention of free riding to trade name owner's good will. The merchant whose trade name is used in said way may seek for termination of confusing business and/or remuneration of damages against junior user.[450] However, in contrast with Trademark Act or Unfair Competition Act, Commercial Act has no special provision to presume damages, which leaves the plaintiff hardship to prove its actual damages in litigations.

445. Commercial Act Art. 18.
446. Commercial Act Art. 20.
447. Commercial Act Art. 22.
448. Commercial Act Art. 23(1).
449. Commercial Act Art. 28.
450. Commercial Act Art. 23(2), (3).

361. Trade name may not be transferred separately from business. The transfer of trade name shall be effective to third party only with registration.[451] Any person who has permitted another person to carry on business using his/her name or trade name shall be liable jointly with such borrowing person to any obligation of transaction with a third party who believed the borrower as actual owner of business.[452] Registered trade name shall be deemed terminated if not used two consecutive years without due reason,[453] and any interested party may seek for the obliteration of such trade name registration.[454]

451. Commercial Act Art. 25.
452. Commercial Act Art. 24.
453. Commercial Act Art. 26.
454. Commercial Act Art. 27.

Chapter 6. Industrial Designs

§1. Source: Legislation

362. In contrast with legislations that categorize design a type of patent, in Korea, design is regulated as separate subcategory of industrial intellectual property. Design Protection Act was enacted initially on 31 December 1961 and has been amended for thirty-five times as of January 2014. Korea joined Locarno Agreement Establishing an International Classification for Industrial Designs in April 2011.

§2. Subject Matter of Protection

I. Design as Subject Matter

363. 'Design' means the shape, pattern, colour, or a combination thereof which are expressed on an article producing aesthetic impression.[455]

II. Requirement of Registration

364. To be protected as a design right, the design shall meet following requirements and registered in Korea.

A. Article

365. The design shall be embodied in an article, which is two dimensional or three-dimensional things of fixed form. Generally, the article implies single corporeal movables, while the exceptions of 'partial design' and 'design as a set' exist.

B. Shape, Pattern, and Colour

366. 'Shape' refers to the contour of three-dimensional articles. 'Pattern' means any dot, line, drawing, apparent, or blurred division line between colours on the surface of articles. 'Design' as a subject matter of Design Protection Act refers to article's shape, pattern, colour, or combinations thereof.

C. Aesthetic Impression in Visuality

367. Design shall have aesthetic impression in visuality. The visual impression must be something perceived instantly from the article. Thus, if the design element

455. DA Art. 2. 1.

is laid inside of an article and destruction or disassembly of article is necessary for perception, such is not subject design of Act.

III. Special Types of Design in Statute

A. Partial Design

368. Though it is principle that the design shall be of single article, the part of an article may be protected as 'partial design' if it constitutes independent unit of aesthetic value.[456]

B. Typeface

369. As typeface is a set of one or more fonts each composed of glyphs that share common design features, it is not 'article' as it is. Nonetheless, Design Protection Act takes typeface as subject matter of protection.[457]

C. Design as a Set of Goods

370. Where two or more goods are used as a set (e.g., spoons and forks, cup and saucers) the design of such goods may be registered in one. The goods entitled to this type of design are enumerated in Enforcement Rule of Design Protection Act.

§3. Conditions of Protection

I. General Conditions of Registration

371. Design must be registered to be protected under Design Protection Act. Articles 33 and 34 provide the conditions of registration as the followings.[458]

A. Industrial Applicability

372. Design shall be applicable on goods industrially reproducible. For such reason, industrial applicability is negated for agricultural products and works of fine arts.

456. DA Art. 2. 1.
457. DA Art. 2. 2.
458. DA Art. 33(1).

B. Novelty

1. General Rule

373. Where the design filed for registration is same or similar with any design disclosed to public before its filing date, such design shall not be registered. The alternative causes of public disclosure are that:

(1) The same or similar design was publicly used in Korea or foreign country.
(2) The same or similar design was printed in any publication in Korea or foreign country.
(3) The same or similar design was exhibited on the internet.[459]

2. Non-prejudicial Disclosures[460]

374. Where a design is disclosed before filing date, the applicant may claim within six months as of filing date that he/she is the creator or lawful successor of disclosed design. If it is the case, such design is not deemed prior design to defeat novelty or nonobviousness of filed design, unless the disclosure was made as filed or registered design in official gazettes. The applicant to claim non-prejudicial disclosure shall submit relevant documents within statutory period.

C. Nonobviousness

1. Obviousness from Known Design(s)[461]

375. Where a person having ordinary creativity in the field of pertinent design (hereinafter referred as 'ordinary designer') could create the design easily from any of:

(1) The design publicly used in Korea or foreign country before filing date.
(2) The design printed in any publication in Korea or foreign country before filing date.
(3) The design exhibited on the internet before filing date.
(4) The combination of designs enumerated above.

Such design is unqualified for registration as it is obvious.

459. DA Art. 33(1) 1., 2.
460. DA Art. 36.
461. DA Art. 33(2) 1.

2. Obviousness from Conventional Design(s)[462]

376. The design is unregistrable where an ordinary designer could create the design easily from the conventional shape, pattern, colour, or the combination thereof before filing date. It is the same where 'known design' is combined to 'conventional design'. The examples of conventional design are, triangle, square, circle, star, oblique lines, cross stripes, globular shape, triangular prism, square pillar, cylinder, typical shapes of natural or artificial things (fish, bird, airplane, car, building, etc.); typical snap motions of human(s) or animal(s), etc.

II. Negative Conditions[463]

377. For the purpose of public interest, Design Protection Act enumerates following designs unregistrable:

(1) Designs same or similar with public identifications such as, national flag, national emblem, military flags, decorations, orders of merit, badges and medals of public organizations, national flags and national emblems of foreign countries, or characters or indications of international organizations.
(2) Designs whose meanings, contents, etc., are likely to cause an offence to public morality that represents the normal moral sense of the public, or disrupt public order.
(3) Designs which possibly cause confusion with respect to articles connected with another person's business.
(4) Designs consisting solely of a shape that is indispensable to secure the functions of the article.

§4. Formalities (Procedure for Grant and Obtaining Protection)

I. General

378. As with patent and trademark, the applicant of design registration shall submit filing document to KIPO.[464] The examiner shall decide registration unless he/she locates any cause of unregistrablity through examination.[465] Where the design was created jointly, the application shall be made in whole joint workers' name.[466] Each application shall be made for each design and multiple designs shall not be filed in single application.[467] However, this doctrine is applied very leniently in practice. As aforementioned, the articles ordinarily used as a set may be applied

462. DA Art. 33(2) 2.
463. DA Art. 34.
464. DA Art. 37.
465. DA Art. 65.
466. DA Art. 39.
467. DA Art. 40(1).

and registered as a unit of design.[468] Further, the Act provides another exception of 'Group Design', which is explained below. The application shall be made in accordance with classification of designs in Enforcement Rule of Design Protection Act.[469]

Where two or more applications for the same or similar design are filed on different date, the application of previous date has priority (first to file doctrine).[470] Where two or more applications for the same or a similar design are filed on a date, only one person agreed upon by all applicants after consultation may obtain registration for the design and, if no agreement is reached or no consultation is possible, none of the applicants shall obtain the registration.[471]

II. Special Types of Applications in Statute

A. *Relevant Design*[472]

379. Any design right owner or applicant may make subsequent application for a design similar to priorly registered or applied ones in the name of 'relevant design'. The subsequent design must be similar only to priorly applied or registered ones.[473] Principally, the priorly filed or registered design shall trigger first to file issue or novelty issue, preventing registration of later design. However, the Act provides exceptional rule to allow the right owner or applicant to obtain rights on series of similar designs. The duration of relevant design right depends on the prior design right and they expire on the same date.[474]

B. *Secret Design*[475]

380. Secret design refers to a design the substance of which is undisclosed for a period time after application. Many designs in the market are vulnerable to imitation and tend to have short span of competitiveness, being susceptible to fashion. Without any alternative to keep applied design as secret, the competitors may learn the design from gazette and sell imitated articles in the market even prior to the applicant. Design Protection Act provides secret design rule to cope with this possibility, protecting applicant from such unfair practice. Applicant may request the substance of his/her design to be kept secret for three years maximum as from registration date. The substance of secret design shall not be printed in gazette in spite of its registration for aforesaid period. The commissioner of KIPO may not allow

468. DA Art. 42.
469. DA Art. 40(2).
470. DA Art. 46(1).
471. DA Art. 46(2).
472. DA Art. 35.
473. DA Art. 35(1).
474. DA Art. 91(1), proviso.
475. DA Art. 43.

the public to review the substance of secret design unless it falls on exceptional cases enumerated in Article 43(4).

C. Group Design[476]

381. As aforementioned, it is principle that an application shall be made for a design. Nonetheless, considering the reality that many variations of design stem from the main idea, the Act allows the registration of multiple designs in a single application. For entitlement of group design, the designs shall belong to same classification in Enforcement Rule of Design Protection Act. Up to 100 designs may be applied together as 'Group Design'.

III. Specialties of Design Protection Act in Application and Examination

382. Most procedural rules for registration of design are same with those of patent. Thus, most of procedural issue in patent prosecution can be referred to the process of design. The special rules of design prosecution worthy of note are as the followings.

A. The Principle of Disclosure upon Request

383. In contrast with patent application, which is disclosed compulsorily after eighteen months of application, the applied design is not disclosed before registration unless the applicant requires disclosure voluntarily.[477] This is because the necessity to conceal substance of applied design is strong due to vulnerability to imitations and short life span. Once the applicant requests disclosure, the Commissioner of KIPO discloses pertinent design by publication of gazette.

B. Registration by Partial Examination

1. Definition

384. 'Partial Examination' means the examination conducted by restricted elements in full checklist.[478] For design, considering its short life span, the early registration is strong demands of many applicants. Design Protection Act reflects this reality providing 'easy registration coupled with post grant review' rule. According to Article 37(4), the applicant of certain designs[479] may request partial examination when making application. In that case, the examiner's list of examination is limited to:[480]

476. DA Art. 41.
477. DA Art. 52(1).
478. DA Art. 2. 6.
479. The designs entitled to partial examination are enumerated in Enforcement Rule.
480. DA Art. 62(2).

(1) If the application is derived by unlawful party.
(2) If the foreign applicant has capacity to enjoy right under domestic law.
(3) If the design has industrial applicability.
(4) If the design is obvious for ordinary designer to derive from conventional design(s).
(5) If the design falls on negative conditions of registration in Article 34.
(6) If the design is of goods suitable for partial examination according to statute.
(7) If the design meets each and every requirement of, joint application; an application for a design; group application; application as a set.
(8) If the application is against Treaty.

2. Post Grant Review

385. Any third party may make an objection against registration on partial examination within three months as from the publication of such registration.[481] The objection shall be reviewed by the panel of three examiners, and if the objection is deemed to have ground, the decision of registration is to be cancelled.[482] The cancellation has retroactive effect.[483]

§5. Ownership and Transfer (Assignment: Licenses)

I. Establishment and Transfer of Design Right

386. Design right is established with registration.[484] Design right is transferrable, but the original design and its relevant design shall be transferred in a unit to a same person only.[485] The transfer and establishment of pledge shall obtain effectiveness with registration.[486] Where design right is joint-owned, the share of right shall be transferrable only with unanimous agreement of all joint owners.[487]

II. License

387. The owner of design right may establish exclusive or non-exclusive license to third party. The establishment of exclusive license must be registered to obtain effect.[488] Where the design right is joint-owned, the establishment of license must be under unanimous agreement of all joint owners to be effective.[489] The licensee

481. DA Art. 68(1).
482. DA Art. 73(3).
483. DA Art. 73(4).
484. DA Art. 90(1).
485. DA Art. 96(1).
486. DA Art. 98(1).
487. DA Art. 96(2).
488. DA Art. 98(1) 2.
489. DA Art. 97(5); DA Art. 99(6).

may not transfer, establish pledge right or sub-license his/her license without consent of design right holder.[490] In contrast with exclusive license, which obtains in rem effect with registration, non-exclusive license has only contractual effect between right holder and licensee. However, once registered, the non-exclusive license shall be effective against subsequent assignee or exclusive licensee of design right.[491]

§6. Scope of Exclusive Rights

388. The owner of design right shall have exclusive right to use the same or similar design with his/her registered design.[492] It is to be noted that the exclusive right of design extends to realm of similarity. The scope of protection of a registered design shall be determined by, the description in an application; drawing and photograph attached; the explanation in the sample or drawing.[493] Where a design is same or similar with another person's priorly applied and registered design, the owner of design right shall obtain consent of said prior design to use his/her design commercially. It is the same where a part of registered design is using priorly applied and registered design of another person.[494]

§7. Limitations of the Scope of Protection

I. Scope to Which Effect of Design Right Is Not Extended[495]

389. The effect of a design right shall not extend to any of the following:

(1) Working of a registered design for the purpose of research or experiment.
(2) Vessels, aircraft, or vehicles merely passing through Korea, or the machinery, instruments, equipment, or other things used therein.
(3) Things existed in Korea before an application was filed.

390. Where a font is registered as a design right, the effect of such right shall not extend to any of the following:

(1) When the font is used in ordinary process, such as typing, typesetting, printing, etc.
(2) Materials produced by use of the font.

490. DA Art. 97(3), (4); DA Art. 99(4), (5).
491. DA Art. 104(1).
492. DA Art. 92.
493. DA Art. 93.
494. DA Art. 95(1), (2).
495. DA Art. 94.

II. Prior User's Right[496]

391. Non-exclusive license to a registered design is conferred on a person satisfying all of following conditions, namely:

(1) The person created or learned the substance of design in good faith before filing date of registered design.
(2) The person began business or preparation of business in Korea based upon such design.
(3) Said prior design is same or similar with registered design.

§8. Duration of Protection

392. Once the decision of registration is noticed, the applicant shall pay registration fee.[497] With such payment, the Commissioner of KIPO shall register the design. The duration period of registered design is twenty years as from filing date.[498] Design right may be abandoned and it expires immediately with abandonment.[499] Meanwhile, the right holder shall obtain consent of licensee before abandonment if he/she have established license on it.[500]

§9. Infringement and Remedies

I. Infringement

A. Original Type of Infringement

393. The owner of design right has exclusive right to use design in business.[501] Thus, it constitutes infringement if any other person uses same or similar design commercially without consent. The 'use' here refers to any act of manufacturing, using, assigning, leasing, exporting, importing, or offering for assignment or lease of (including displaying for the purpose of assignment or lease) an article to which a design has been applied.[502]

496. DA Art. 100.
497. DA Art. 79.
498. DA Art. 91.
499. DA Art. 107.
500. DA Art. 106.
501. DA Art. 92.
502. DA Art. 2. 7.

B. *Deeds Regarded as Infringement (Indirect Infringement)*[503]

394. Deeds of commercially manufacturing, assigning, leasing, exporting, importing or offering for assigning, or leasing articles are deemed infringement where:

(1) Such articles have no other use but manufacturing goods of a certain design, and
(2) said design is same or similar with registered design of another person.

The norm of this provision is same with 'indirect infringement' in Patent Act. Namely, to prevent any physical aid of direct infringement, protecting design right more substantially and aggressively.

II. Remedies

A. *Prohibition Order (Injunction)*[504]

395. An owner of a design right or exclusive licensee may demand a person who is infringing or is likely to infringe on his/her rights to discontinue or prevent such infringement. Infringer's subjective conditions of wilfulness or negligence are not considered for prohibition order. The right holder of secret design may demand prohibition order only after warning with document authorized by the Commissioner of KIPO where the substance of design is included.[505] This is because the substance of design is unknown in secret design and the alleged infringer cannot perceive if the demander is authentic right holder and if his/her work of design constitutes infringement.

B. *Damages*

396. Infringement of design right is an act of 'tort'. Damages are available to torts of wilfulness or negligence in accordance with relevant provisions in Civil Act.[506] However, in most cases, it is hard for plaintiff to prove causal relation between infringement and 'actual damages'. To alleviate this problem and protect plaintiff effectively, Design Protection Act provides several special articles of damage calibration rules, which are based upon some legal presumptions.

503. DA Art. 114.
504. DA Art. 113.
505. DA Art. 113(2).
506. Civil Act, Art. 750.

1. 'Number of Transferred Articles by Infringer X 'Right Holder's Profit per Unit'

397. In measuring damages, the amount of losses may be calculated by multiplying 'the number of articles infringer transferred' by 'the right holder's possible profit per unit of the article'.[507] In such cases, the compensation shall be determined between the amount that right holder's total capability of sales would have produced as maximum, and the amount that right holder actually has sold under circumstance of infringement. Where defendant successfully attests the amount that plaint would not have obtained even without infringement, such amount shall be deducted from aforesaid damage amount. The burden of proof about such situation goes to defendant.[508]

2. Presumption of Infringer's Profit to Damages

398. If infringer has gained any profit by infringement, the relevant amount of profit shall be presumed to be the amount of damages sustained by design right holder.[509] As with Article 115(2), this provision is regarded applicable only where the right holder produces or sales goods by himself/herself. However, it is generally hard for plaintiff to prove 'profit' of defendant.

3. Reasonable Royalty

399. Plaintiff may choose the amount of reasonable royalty as damages against design right infringement.[510] For the damages of Article 115(1) or (3), the court may exercise its discretion, deducting the amount, if not wilful infringement or of gross negligence.[511] In contrast with it, there is no space of discretion and the reasonable royalty is guaranteed as base amount of damages for infringement. The 'reasonable royalty' here denotes objective amount of money, which would have been paid if infringer had gone into a license contract with right holder. If any case of prior license exists, the actual amount of royalty may be standard; if no such case exists, the practical royalty in the field of work will be criteria deciding reasonable royalty.

4. Decision of Damages by Discretion

400. Where it is difficult to decide damages by Article 115(1) through (4), court may fix considerable damages on its discretion in the light of total purport and

507. DA Art. 115(1).
508. DA Art. 115(2).
509. DA Art. 115(3).
510. DA Art. 115(4).
511. DA Art. 115(5).

evidence in litigation.[512] This is supplemental rule provided for plaintiff who evidently suffered damages by infringement but eventually failed to prove any of its amounts.

5. Presumption of Negligence

401. Where any person infringes registered design right, his/her negligence in infringement is presumed. However, such presumption rule is not applied to infringement of secret design.[513]

III. Return of Unjust Enrichment

402. Design right holder may seek for return of unjust enrichment caused by infringement selectively with damages. The option of 'return of unjust enrichment' is merited for plaintiff in light of extinctive prescription (long term of ten years, while that of damages is short term of three years). On the other hand, there is no applicability of presumption rules of Article 115; plaintiff bears heavy burden of proof for causation between infringement and defendant's enrichment.

IV. Recovery of Reputation

403. Upon request of a design right holder, court may order the infringer who has injured the business reputation of right holder to take necessary measures to restore business reputation.[514]

V. Criminal Sanctions

404. In Korea, design right infringements are subject to criminal sanctions of imprisonment or fine. Any person who has infringed a design right or an exclusive license shall be punished by imprisonment for not more than seven years or by a fine not exceeding KRW 100 million.[515]

512. DA Art. 115(6).
513. DA Art. 116.
514. DA Art. 117.
515. DA Art. 220.

§10. Overlapping and Relation to Other Intellectual Property Law

405. Copyright act defines:

> 'Works of applied art' is artistic works that may be copied on the goods in the same shapes, and whose originality may be recognized apart from the relevant applied goods, and that include designs, etc.[516]

As stipulated in the article, Copyright Act renders overlapped protection for industrial design with Design Protection Act. Supreme Court cases once ruled that the applied arts are protected only by Design Protection Act unless they bear 'outstanding artistic value'. However, the Supreme Court has changed its attitude toward capability of double protection.[517] To be obtained, copyright requires no formality other than creation, while design protection requires examination and registration. Duration periods of each right differs: author's lifetime and seventy years after death for copyright, twenty years after filing date for registered design. Most of all, the design must have novelty and nonobviousness against any prior design disclosed before its filing date. On the other hand, the existence of same or similar work in prior does not automatically negate copyright unless the junior worker has copied it.

§11. Trials Relevant to Design Right

406. The major types of trials Design Protection Act provides are Trial to Appeal the Rejection (Article 120), Invalidation Trial (Article 121), and Trial to Confirm the Scope of Right (Article 122). As most substance of those is analogous with patent trials, such may be referred to.

516. CA. Art 2. 15.
517. SCt. 2004. 7. 22. – 2003 Do 7572.

Chapter 7. Plant Variety Protection

§1. Sources: Legislation

407. In accordance with TRIPs 27.3 (b),[518] Korea enacted Seed Industry Act in December 1995 to provide protection for plant variety. Afterwards, Korea joined International Union for the Protection of New Varieties of Plants (in January 2002), and enacted New Varieties of Plants Protection Act in 1 June 2012, which began enforcement as of 2 June 2013. Korea confers patent protection on inventions of sexual/asexual propagation plants, and separate protection of breeder's right on new variety of plants, which are registered. The procedure for registration and substance of protection for plant variety under New Varieties of Plants Protection Act is briefly described below.

§2. Subject Matter of Protection

408. All plant genera and species are subject matters of New Varieties of Plants Protection Act.[519]

§3. Conditions of Protection

I. Novelty[520]

409. The variety shall be deemed new if propagating or harvested material of the variety has not been sold or disposed of to others, with the consent of the breeder, for purposes of exploitation of the variety:

(1) In Korea, earlier than one year before the filing date.
(2) In countries other than Korea, earlier than four years (in the case of trees or of vines, earlier than six years) before the filing date.

II. Distinctness[521]

410. The variety shall be deemed distinct if it is clearly distinguishable from any other variety whose existence is a matter of common knowledge at the time of filing application. 'Matter of common knowledge' here includes:

(1) Variety in distribution.
(2) Variety protected by breeder's right or applied for breeder's right.

518. TRIPs 27.3 (b) requires Member States to protect plant variety by patent or special Act or combination thereof.
519. New Varieties of Plants Protection Act (Hereinafter, NVPPA), Art. 3.
520. NVPPA. Art. 17.
521. NVPPA. Art. 18.

(3) Variety registered in official list or applied for registration.

III. Uniformity[522]

411. The variety shall be deemed uniform if, subject to the variation that may be expected from the particular features of its propagation, it is sufficiently uniform in its relevant characteristics.

IV. Stability[523]

412. The variety shall be deemed stable if its relevant characteristics remain unchanged after repeated propagation or, in the case of a particular cycle of propagation, at the end of each such cycle.

V. Denomination[524]

413. Variety under application shall have its original denomination. The detailed requisites of valid denomination are listed in Article 107.

§4. Formalities (Procedure for Grant and Obtaining Protection)

I. Application

414. The breeder and the legitimate successor has right to file for registration.[525] If applications compete on identical variety, the application filed on prior date is qualified for registration.[526] The right to seek for registration can be transferred by contract.[527] Application shall be filed to Minister of Agriculture, Food and Rural Affairs or Minister of Oceans and Fisheries.[528] The filing document shall contain: (1) name and address of breeder, (2) scientific name and general name of the variety, (3) denomination of the variety, (4) filing date, (5) explanation of the character and breeding process of the variety, (6) photo of variety, and (7) sample of seed, etc.[529]

---

522. NVPPA. Art. 19.
523. NVPPA. Art. 20.
524. NVPPA. Art. 16. 5; Art. 106.
525. NVPPA. Art. 21.
526. NVPPA. Art. 25.
527. NVPPA. Art. 26.
528. NVPPA. Art. 30(1).
529. NVPPA. Art. 30(1), (2).

II. Examination

415. The registrability of filed application shall be screened by the examiner. Examiner shall screen the novelty, distinctness, uniformity, and stability of filed variety.[530] Minister of Agriculture, Food and Rural Affairs, or Minister of Oceans and Fisheries ought to disclose information of filed variety immediately through gazette.[531] After the publication, any person may submit opposition to foresaid ministers directing reasons and offering information to make filed variety unregistrable.[532] In the course of the examination, the authority may grow the variety or carry out other necessary tests other than documentary examination.[533] For the purposes of examination, the authority may require the breeder to furnish all the necessary information, documents, or material.[534]

III. Provisional Protection

416. Applicant may exclusively enjoy the breeder's right from the date of disclosure publication.[535] Under this provisional right, applicant is entitled to remuneration from any person who carries out acts which require breeder's authorization if the variety is registered. Said provisional right disappears retroactively once rejection to the application is confirmed.[536]

IV. Decision of Registration

417. If no reason of rejection is found, examiner ought to render a decision of registration for the filed variety and publish it in gazette after the notice to applicant.[537]

§5. Ownership and Transfer (Assignment: Licenses)

I. Assignment

418. Breeder's right is established with its registration.[538] Breeder's right is transferrable,[539] and the transfer and establishment of pledge shall obtain

530. NVPPA. Art. 40(1).
531. NVPPA. Art. 37(1).
532. NVPPA. Art. 37(2).
533. NVPPA. Art. 40(3); NVPPA. Enforcement Rule Art. 47.
534. NVPPA. Art. 41.
535. NVPPA. Art. 38(1).
536. NVPPA. Art. 38(2).
537. NVPPA. Art. 43.
538. NVPPA. Art. 54(1).
539. NVPPA. Art. 60(1).

effectiveness with registration.[540] Where breeder's right is joint-owned, the share of right shall be transferrable only with unanimous agreement of whole joint owners.[541]

II. License

419. The owner of breeder's right may establish exclusive/non-exclusive license.[542] The exclusive license has in rem effect and the licensee may seek for remedies against infringer in his/her name.[543] Non-exclusive license has only contractual effect between licensor and licensee, and licensee may not seek for remedies against infringer in his/her name, while he/she can demand licensor to exercise such rights on behalf of him/her. Further, non-exclusive licensee may not assert his license to subsequent assignee or exclusive licensee of breeder's right, whereas he/she may assert said license after it is registered.[544] Non-exclusive license may be established by statute,[545] or by order of government authority.[546]

§6. Scope of Exclusive Rights

420. Breeder's right holder has exclusive right to work the breed.[547] 'Work' here refers to:

(1) Production or reproduction (multiplication).
(2) Conditioning for the purpose of propagation.
(3) Sale, rental, or other marketing.
(4) Offering for sale or rental.
(5) Exporting, importing.
(6) Exhibition for sale or rental.[548]

Breeder's right extends to the harvested material and any product made directly from the harvested material, once it is enabled by unauthorized use of propagating material of protected variety.[549]

540. NVPPA. Art. 62.
541. NVPPA. Art. 66(1), (2).
542. NVPPA. Art. 61(1).
543. NVPPA. Art. 83(1).
544. NVPPA. Art. 74(1).
545. NVPPA. Arts 64; 65; 66.
546. NVPPA. Art. 67.
547. NVPPA. Art. 56(1).
548. NVPPA. Art. 2. 7.
549. NVPPA. Art. 56(2).

§7. LIMITATIONS OF THE SCOPE OF PROTECTION

I. Scope to Which Effect of Breeder's Right Is Not Extended

421. The breeder's right shall not extend to:

(1) Acts done privately and for non-commercial purposes;
(2) Acts done for experimental purposes;
(3) Acts done for the purpose of breeding other varieties.[550]

II. Exhaustion

422. The breeder's right shall not extend to acts concerning any material of the protected variety which has been sold or otherwise marketed by the breeder or licensee in Korea. 'Material' here means: (1) propagating material, and (2) harvested material or any product made directly from the harvested material. This rule does not apply for: (1) further propagation of variety using said material, and (2) exporting material for the purpose of propagation.[551]

§8. DURATION OF PROTECTION

423. The protection period for breeder's right is twenty years from registration date. Protection period for trees and vines is twenty-five years.[552]

§9. INFRINGEMENT AND REMEDIES

I. Prohibition Order (Injunction)[553]

424. An owner of a breeder's right or exclusive licensee may demand a person who is infringing or is likely to infringe on his/her rights to discontinue or prevent such infringement.

II. Acts Deemed Infringement

425. In addition to the act of unauthorized use of registered variety, unauthorized use of identical or similar denomination to other plant that belongs to same genus or species with registered variety is deemed infringement.[554]

550. NVPPA. Art. 57(1) 1., 2., 3.
551. NVPPA. Art. 58.
552. NVPPA. Art. 55.
553. NVPPA. Art. 83.
554. NVPPA. Art. 84.

III. Damages

426. For damages from breeder's right infringement, the relevant provisions of patent shall apply *mutatis mutandis*.[555] Accordingly, the description in patent infringement and damages may be referred to. The infringer of registered breeder's right is deemed to have negligence.[556]

IV. Recovery of Reputation

427. Upon request of a breeder's right holder, court may order the infringer who has injured the business reputation of right holder to take necessary measures to restore the business reputation.[557]

V. Criminal Sanctions

428. In Korea, breeder's right infringements are entitled to criminal sanctions of imprisonment or fine. Any person who has infringed a breeder's right or an exclusive license shall be punished by imprisonment for not more than seven years or by a fine not exceeding KRW 100 million.[558]

§10. Overlapping and Relation to Other Intellectual Property Laws

429. Other than Plant Variety Act, any sexually and asexually propagating plants may be protected under Patent Act as long as it suffices the conditions of invention and patentability. KIPO examines and grants patent to such inventions under biotechnology examination guidelines.[559]

§11. Trials Relevant to Breeder's Right

430. Major trials relevant to breeder's right are Trial of Appeal to Rejection (Article 91) and Invalidation Trial (Article 92). For most procedural elements, the pertinent provisions of Patent Act are applied *mutatis mutandis*.[560]

555. NVPPA. Art. 85(2).
556. NVPPA. Art. 86.
557. NVPPA. Art. 87.
558. NVPPA. Art. 131.
559. KIPO, Patent Examination Guidelines (2013), Part IX. Ch. 1.
560. NVPPA. Art. 98.

Chapter 8. Chip Protection

§1. Sources: Legislation

431. Act On the Layout-Designs of Semiconductor Integrated Circuits (hereinafter referred to as 'Semiconductor Act') is the source of law for chip protection in Korea. Semiconductor Act was initially enacted in 8 December 1992 and amended eleven times as of January 2014.

§2. Subject Matter of Protection

432. Subject matter of Semiconductor Act is the layout-design of creative semiconductor integrated circuit. The term 'semiconductor integrated circuit' means a semi-finished or finished product that has been manufactured to function as an electronic circuit. Such circuit shall consist of circuit elements including one or more active elements and wires connecting such elements. They shall be laid onto the surface of any semiconductor or insulating material, or into semiconductor material, in an inseparable form.[561] The term 'layout-design' means a design laying out various circuit elements and connecting wires in two or three dimensions in order to manufacture a semiconductor integrated circuit.[562] The standard of 'creativity' is rather lenient and is met only if not ordinary.[563]

§3. Conditions of Protection

433. Layout-design rights subsist as from the date of registration.[564] In contrast with patent, trademark, and design, layout-design is registered without examination but the check of formalities.

§4. Formalities (Procedure for Grant and Obtaining Protection)

I. Application for Registration

434. Any person who has created a layout-design or lawful successor may apply for registration at KIPO within two years from the date on which the layout-design was initially used in commercial purpose.[565]

561. Semiconductor Act. Art. 2.1.
562. Semiconductor Act. Art. 2.2.
563. Semiconductor Act. Art. 2.3.
564. Semiconductor Act. Art. 6.
565. Semiconductor Act. Art. 19.

II. Rejection of Applications

435. The Commissioner of KIPO shall reject the application in either case where:

(1) The applicant is not the creator.
(2) The application was not made under the name of all members in spite that the right is joint-owned.
(3) The time period for application has elapsed.
(4) Any accompanying document required for the application has not been submitted or any other ground exists as specified by Presidential Decree.[566]

III. Registration of Creation and Public Notices[567]

436. The Commissioner of KIPO shall upon receiving an application, register the creation of the layout-design unless the application has defect enumerated in Article 20(1). When the registration is complete, the Commissioner shall issue a certificate to the holder of the layout-design right and issue public notice thereof.

IV. Cancellation of Registered Rights[568]

437. The Commissioner may cancel the registration in either case where:

(1) The registration violates a treaty under Article 3(1)
(2) The registration of creation under Article 21(1) has been made by deceit or in any other fraudulent way.

The Commissioner must cancel the registration in either case where:

(1) The registration has been made by deceit or in any other fraudulent way
(2) The layout-design falls under any of Article 20(1) 1 through 3.

§5. Ownership and Transfer (Assignment: Licenses)

I. Establishment and Assignment

438. Layout-design subsists as from the registration, and is transferable.[569] If a layout-design right is owned by joint owners, each joint owner shall obtain unanimous consent of other shareholders to transfer or pledge his/her share to third

566. Semiconductor Act. Art. 20.
567. Semiconductor Act. Art. 21.
568. Semiconductor Act. Art. 24.
569. Semiconductor Act. Art. 10(1).

party.[570] The transfer and establishment of pledge must be recorded to have third party effect.[571]

II. License

A. *Exclusive License*

439. A layout-design right holder may grant another person an exclusive license.[572] Exclusive licensee may seek for injunctive relief and damages against infringer by his/her own name.[573]

B. *Non-exclusive License*

440. Non-exclusive license is a contractual right that the licensor allows licensee to use layout-design and refrain from exercising injunction against such use. Thus, the licensee has no right to seek for injunctive relief or damages in his/her own name against infringer. Once the license is registered, non-exclusive licensee may assert his/her right to third party who succeed or obtained exclusive right for layout-design right.[574]

§6. Scope of Exclusive Rights

441. The layout-design right holder shall have exclusive right to use the layout-design for profit.[575] The term 'use' means any of the following activities:[576]

(1) Reproducing layout-design.
(2) Manufacturing of a semiconductor integrated circuit based on a layout-design.
(3) Transferring, leasing, displaying (limited to purpose of assignment or lease), or importing, a layout-design; a semiconductor integrated circuit manufactured according to a layout-design; a product manufactured by applying a semiconductor integrated circuit (hereinafter, referred to as 'lay-out design etc.').

If a layout-design right is owned by joint owners, each joint owner has a right to use the layout-design without the other joint holders' consent, unless there is a specific agreement to the contrary.[577]

570. Semiconductor Act. Art. 10(3).
571. Semiconductor Act. Art. 23.
572. Semiconductor Act. Art. 11.
573. Semiconductor Act. Art. 35(1); Semiconductor Act. Art. 36(1).
574. Semiconductor Act. Art. 23(2).
575. Semiconductor Act. Art. 6.
576. Semiconductor Act. Art. 2-4.
577. Semiconductor Act. Art. 10(4).

§7. LIMITATIONS OF THE SCOPE OF PROTECTION

I. Limitations of Scope of Layout-Design Rights[578]

442. The layout-design right shall not extend to any of the following:

(1) A layout-design reproduced directly or vicariously, for education, research, analysis, evaluation, or any other similar activities or for personal use for any non-profit purpose.
(2) A creative layout-design produced as a result of research, analysis, evaluation, or any other similar activities under subparagraph (1).
(3) An independent creative layout-design produced by another person, which is identical with registered lay-out design.

II. Exhaustion

443. Where the lay-out design circuit was lawfully assigned by right holder, the layout-design right does not extend to, transferring, leasing, displaying, or importing lay-out design etc.[579]

III. Immunity for Bona Fide Person

444. Where a third party of bona fide was assigned of lay-out design etc., which was reproduced unlawfully, the lay-out design right does not extend to transferring, leasing, displaying (limited to purpose of assignment or lease), or importing such lay-out design etc., by such third party.[580]

IV. Adjudication on Non-exclusive License Grant

445. Semiconductor Act stipulates adjudication of non-exclusive license by The Commissioner of KIPO. The detailed conditions for such adjudication and its procedures are provided in Article 13.

§8. DURATION OF PROTECTION

446. The duration of a layout-design right is ten years from the registration date.[581] However, such duration shall not exceed: (1) ten years from initial commercial use of lay-out design, and (2) fifteen years from the date of creation.[582]

578. Semiconductor Act. Art. 9.
579. Semiconductor Act. Art. 9(2).
580. Semiconductor Act. Art. 9(3).
581. Semiconductor Act. Art. 7(1).
582. Semiconductor Act. Art. 7(2).

§9. INFRINGEMENT AND REMEDIES

I. Prohibition Order (Injunction)[583]

447. The layout-design right holder or exclusive licensee has a right to demand a person who infringed or is likely to infringe the right to cease such infringement or take preventive measures.

II. Damages

A. General

448. The layout-design right holder or exclusive licensee may claim any person who infringes the right by intention or negligence to compensate his/her losses.[584]

B. Presumption of Infringer's Profit as Damages

449. If infringer has gained any profit by infringement, the relevant amount of profit shall be presumed to be the amount of damages sustained by right holder.[585]

C. Reasonable Royalty

450. Plaintiff may choose the amount of reasonable royalty as damages against lay-out design right infringement.[586] The 'reasonable royalty' here denotes objective amount of money, which would have been paid if infringer had gone into a license contract with right holder. If any case of prior license exists, the actual amount of royalty may be standard; if no such case exists, the practical royalty in the field of work will be criteria deciding reasonable royalty.

III. Unauthorized User's Duty of Compensation for the Use Prior to Registration

451. The creator of a layout-design who had commercially used the layout-design before registration may claim any person who commercially used a reproduction of such layout-design after creator's use. The compensation shall be equivalent to reasonable royalty for unauthorized use through registration date. Such compensation may not be claimed against a person who has received, in good

583. Semiconductor Act. Art. 35.
584. Semiconductor Act. Art. 36(1).
585. Semiconductor Act. Art. 36(2).
586. Semiconductor Act. Art. 36(3).

faith and without negligence, circuit or similar product manufactured and delivered by using a reproduction of the layout-design.[587]

§10. OVERLAPPING AND RELATION TO OTHER INTELLECTUAL PROPERTY LAWS

452. Regarding the right is granted to design which meets minimum standard of creativity without further examination, the lay-out design has a nature similar to copyright. On the other hand, in the aspect that the right is granted through registration and can be cancelled by post grant review of creativity,[588] the lay-out design also has a nature similar to patent. Practically, the Chip Protection Act applies many of Patent Act provisions *mutatis mutandis*.[589]

587. Semiconductor Act. Art. 37.
588. Semiconductor Act. Art. 24, 3.
589. Semiconductor Act. Art. 5-2.

Chapter 9. Trade Secrets/Confidential Information

§1. Sources: Legislation

453. In Korea, Unfair Competition Act is the source of law to protect trade secret. Unfair Competition Act comprises of provisions to regulate unfair competition and to protect trade secret from unjust disclosure or appropriation by others. In contrast with other countries, which have separate legislation of trade secret protection, Korea regulates unfair competition and trade secret protection with single Act, disposing each rule in distinct Chapters. In 1991, the Chapter of trade secret protection was instituted into Unfair Competition Act (Amended Act No. 4478).

§2. The Protection of Trade Secrets/Confidential Information

I. Definition of Trade Secret

454. To be protected as trade secret, the information shall satisfy all of the following conditions:

(1) Useful one pertinent to technology or management of business;
(2) Unknown to public and has independent economic value;
(3) Subject of considerable effort to maintain its secrecy.[590]

Even where a third party became to know the substance of information, it is still trade secret while obligation of secrecy is imposed to such party. On the other hand, once the obligation is breached and the information is disclosed, it is no longer a trade secret.

Taking account the goal of statute, the information against public order, e.g., method of tax evasion, method of emitting polluted material in secret, etc., shall not be protectable trade secret. Considerable effort to maintain secrecy shall be recognized only where such effort is objectively perceivable by, indicating secrecy in proper means of notification or; limiting accessibility or; imposing duty of secrecy to the ones who make access, etc.[591] Namely, mere intention to keep the information in secret is not enough. Instead, the third party must be able to notice the secrecy and certain degree of actual effort must be invested to keep it in secret.

590. Unfair Competition Act, Art. 2. 2.
591. SCt. 2008. 7. 10 – 2008 Do 3435.

II. Categories of Trade Secret Infringement

A. Lineage of Unfair 'Acquirement'

1. Unfair Acquirement, Use, and Disclosure of Trade Secret[592]

455. The acts of acquiring trade secrets by theft, deception, coercion or other improper means, or subsequently using or disclosing such trade secret belong to this category. Unfair Competition Act regards leaking the information to a third party in secret manner also as disclosure. On the other hand, unveiling the secret through fair 'reverse engineering' is deemed legitimate.

2. Subsequent Acquirement, Use, Disclosure of Unfairly Acquired Trade Secret[593]

456. The acts of acquiring trade secret or using or disclosing them with the knowledge that such trade secret was initially acquired by unfair method constitute this type of infringement. It is the same where the lack of such knowledge was caused by gross negligence.

3. Use or Disclosure of Trade Secret after Acquirement in Good Faith[594]

457. When a person acquired another person's trade secret in good faith, the subsequent use or disclosure of such trade secret constitutes infringement, after he/she came to know that it was trade secret initially acquired unfairly. It is the same where he uses or discloses the trade secret in gross negligence of such situation.

B. Lineage of Unfair 'Disclosure'

1. Unfair Disclosure of Trade Secret[595]

458. Where a person who has duty to keep trade secret discloses or uses trade secret to obtain improper benefits or to damage the owner of the secret, such belongs to this category of infringement. It is the most typical case that an employee is scouted by competing company and subsequently discloses or uses the trade secret for new employer.

592. Unfair Competition Act, Art. 2. 3. (a).
593. Unfair Competition Act, Art. 2. 3. (b).
594. Unfair Competition Act, Art. 2. 3. (c).
595. Unfair Competition Act, Art. 2. 3. (d).

2. The Acquirement, Use, or Disclosure of Unfairly Disclosed Trade Secret[596]

459. Where the trade secret was unfairly disclosed in manner of Article 2. 3. (d), the subsequent acts of acquiring, using, or disclosing such trade secret with knowledge constitutes infringement of this type. It is the same where gross negligence was the cause of such acts. This is to control the party who utilizes trade secret in bad faith or gross negligence after it was disclosed by the breacher of duty of secrecy. In practice, the company, which scouts competing company's employee to obtain trade secret, is often ruled by this provision.

3. Use or Disclosure of Trade Secret after Acquirement in Good faith[597]

460. When a person acquired another person's trade secret in good faith, the subsequent use or disclosure of such trade secret constitutes infringement, after he/she came to know that it was trade secret initially disclosed unfairly. It is the same where he uses or discloses the trade secret in gross negligence of such situation.

III. Remedies for Infringement

A. *Prohibition Order (Injunction)*[598]

461. A person who possesses trade secrets may seek a court prohibition or preventive order against a person who infringes or is likely to infringe trade secrets. As a prohibition, the court may order the suspension of relevant business to the infringer. However, the period of suspension shall not exceed reasonable time for the infringer to unveil the secret by lawful method such as reverse engineering.[599] In addition, the court may order employee who infringed trade secret not to open competing business or be employed by competitor. The period of such order also shall not exceed reasonable length to balance the interest of trade secret owner and personal freedom of employee to have occupation.

B. *Damages Etc.*

462. An infringer of trade secret is liable for damages[600] and the person who acquired another person's trade secret unlawfully is deemed liable regardless that he/she actually used the secret. The unlawful acquirement itself triggers liability by deteriorating economic value of trade secret. The damage rules for unfair competition are consolidated with trade secret infringement in Article 14-2. Thus, the

596. Unfair Competition Act, Art. 2. 3. (e).
597. Unfair Competition Act, Art. 2. 3. (f).
598. Unfair Competition Act, Art. 10.
599. SCt. 2009. 3. 16 – 2008 Ma 1087.
600. Unfair Competition Act, Art. 11.

explanation of Article 14-2 in Unfair Competition Act shall be referred to damages of trade secret infringement. Further, the rule for 'return of unjust enrichment' and 'recovery of reputation'[601] in trade secret infringement is identical with that of unfair competition.

C. *Special Rule for Infringement in Good Faith*[602]

463. Where a person acquired a trade secret without knowledge that it concerned infringement and such lack of knowledge is without gross negligence, he/she may use or disclose the secret within the scope that was eligible at the moment of acquirement.[603] Hence, he/she may use or disclose the secret even after awareness of infringement by right holder's notice, so long as he/she was in good faith at the moment of acquirement.

IV. Criminal Sanctions

464. Acquiring, using, leaking of trade secret to gain unjust profit or harm the right holder are subject to criminal punishments.[604] If such acts are under purpose or knowledge that the trade secret is leaked to be used in foreign country, additional penalty shall be imposed.[605] The attempt, preparation, and conspiracy of such crimes are also punished.[606]

601. Unfair Competition Act, Art. 12.
602. Unfair Competition Act, Art. 13.
603. Ibid.
604. Unfair Competition Act, Art. 18(2).
605. Unfair Competition Act, Art. 18(1).
606. Unfair Competition Act, Art. 18-2; 18-3.

Chapter 10. Geographical Indications and Appellations of Origin

465. In the aspect of intellectual property law, South Korea does not have independent law for geographical indications other than individual regulations in Trademark Act and Unfair Competition Act.[607] The relevant explanations in each Act may be referred to.

607. On the other side, the geographical indications are also ruled in the field of 'administrative law' such as 'Act on Origin Labeling of Agricultural and Fishery Products', etc.

Chapter 11. Unfair Competition

§1. Sources: Legislation

466. In Korea, Unfair Competition Prevention and Trade Secret Act ('Unfair Competition Act') is the source of law to regulate act of unfair competition. In contrast with many other countries to rule unfair competition and trade secret protection by separate Acts, Korea regulates both in single Act, disposing each in distinguished chapters. Along with trademark is categorized as an intellectual property for its value to represent source or good will of business, the subjects of Unfair Competition Act play similar roles in the market, demanding protection as a type of intellectual property. As trade secret issue is explained in Chapter 9, the subjects of unfair competition are to be described below.

467. Unfair Competition Act was enacted initially on 30 December 1961 and has been amended twenty-three times until January 2014. It was amendment of 31 December 1991 (Act No. 4478) that trade secret protection chapter was inserted. Unfair Competition Act covers broader range of subject in comparison with Trademark Act. Any type of business identity domestically well known, e.g., name, trade name, figure of goods, etc., is protected by Unfair Competition Act, whereas only registered mark is subject matter of Trademark Act. Article 15 of Unfair Competition Act reveals its nature as a general rule, stipulating, 'if any provision of Trademark Act is inconsistent with the provisions of Unfair Competition Act, such provisions of the relevant Acts shall preferentially apply.'

§2. Rules of Unfair Competition

I. Statutory Types of Unfair Competition

A. *To Arouse Confusion with Other's Goods or Business*

468. To constitute this type of unfair competition act, such goods or business of another person shall be well known in Korea, whether it is registered or not.

1. Deeds to Confuse Source Identity of Goods[608]

469. Causing confusion with another person's goods conforms to this provision, where the confusion is caused either:

(1) By using similar or identical signs with such person's well-known trade name, trademark, container, package of goods, or any other sign as an indication of goods.

608. Unfair Competition Act, Art. 2. 1. a.

(2) By selling, distributing, importing, or exporting goods on which the signs of (1) are indicated.

Even the mark initially of no distinctiveness shall trigger application of this provision once it is well known to consumers in Korea through continuous use. The requirement of 'well-known in Korea' shall be satisfied where the sign is widely known in a certain local area of Korea.[609] In such case, protection may be geographically restricted only to such area. The confusion here implies not only the confusion for source of goods/service, but also the confusion of sponsorship or economical relationship. Supreme Court admits the possibility of 'post-sale confusion' stipulating, 'even without actual confusion at the moment of initial transaction, Article 2. 1. (a) shall apply if it could cause source confusion among downstream transactors in the future'.[610]

2. Deeds to Cause Confusion with Another Person's Business

470. Causing confusion with another person's commercial facilities or activities conforms to this provision, where the confusion is caused by using identical or similar sign to another person's well-known name, trade name, emblem or any other sign of business.[611] The confusion here denotes not only the confusion for source of service, but also that of sponsorship or economical affiliation.

B. To Damage Distinctiveness or Reputation of Prominent Identification[612]

471. Tarnishing distinctiveness or reputation of another person's identification conforms to this provision, where the tarnishment is caused either:

(1) By using similar or identical signs with such person's well-known trade name, trademark, container, package of goods, or any other sign as an indication of goods or business.
(2) By selling, distributing, importing, or exporting goods on which the signs of (1) are indicated.

This clause is mainly oriented to commercial credit of prominent identification owner, other than consumer's interest. Korea has adopted this rule into Unfair Competition Act by amendment of 3 February 2011, to comply with advice of WIPO. In contrast with other countries' that includes 'blurring' as well as tarnishment of business identification, Unfair Competition Act limits the subject only to tarnishment.

609. SCt. 2012. 5. 9 – 2010 Do 6187.
610. SCt. 2012. 12. 13 – 2011 Do 6797.
611. Unfair Competition Act, Art. 2. 1. (b).
612. Unfair Competition Act, Art. 2. 1. (c).

472. In spite that Article 2.1.(c) stipulates the subject as 'well-known' identification. The identification must be 'prominent'.[613] Prominence here implies that the identification is 'very well-known' to Korean public. Presidential Decree Article 1-2 provides several exceptions of this rule. The use of another person's prominent commercial identity is exempted from tarnishment allegation in either case where:

(1) A mark is used for non-commercial purposes. (2) A mark is used in a news report or commentary .(3) The prior user of such identity continues to use it without any unjust purpose after it became another person's prominent business identity. (4) The use of a mark is deemed consistent with practices of fair commerce.

C. Other Types of Unfair Competition Deeds in Statute

1. False Indication About Origin Place[614]

473. An act that possibly causes public confusion about the origin place of transacted goods either:

(1) By falsely marking the origin place either on goods, in an advertisement, on the trade documents, or in the trade communication.
(2) By selling, distributing, importing, and exporting goods falsely marked with the origin place.

2. Arousing Public Confusion About Place of Production or Process[615]

474. An act that can possibly cause public confusion about the origin place where the goods are produced or processed either:

(1) By falsely marking the origin place of production or process either on the trade documents, or in the trade communication.
(2) By selling, distributing, importing, exporting goods falsely marked with the origin place of production or process.

3. Arousing Misconception About Quality of Goods Etc.[616]

475. Any act to:

(1) Falsely assume another person's goods.
(2) Put the mark to mislead quality, substance, method of manufacture, use, or quantity on the goods.

---

613. SCt. 2004. 5. 14 – 2002 Da 13782.
614. Unfair Competition Act, Art. 2. 1. (d).
615. Unfair Competition Act, Art. 2. 1. (e).
616. Unfair Competition Act, Art. 2. 1. (f).

(3) Advertise to mislead quality, substance, method of manufacture, use, or quantity of goods.
(4) Sell, distribute, import, or export goods using such method or mark.

4. Unjustifiable Use of Mark by Agent[617]

476. With regard to mark registered in Member State of Paris Convention, WTO, or Trademark Treaty, any act where:

(1) The agent or representative uses the identical or similar mark on identical or similar goods without justifiable grounds.
(2) The agent or representative sells, distributes, exports, or imports such goods.

5. Domain Name Registration in Unjust Purpose[618]

477. Registration of domain name, which includes another person's domestically prominent name, trade name, trademark, or other mark, under any of following purpose:

(1) To sell or rent the domain name.
(2) To prevent the lawful holder from registering or using the domain name.
(3) To gain commercial profits.

Where a domain name registration conforms to this provision, the lawful holder of such domain name may seek for damages against domain name squatter.[619] Further, he/she may demand deletion of such domain name as a measure of injunction.[620] Supreme Court determined in a trademark case that trademark right holder shall not demand squatter to transfer domain name to him, while deletion or prohibition of use is allowable as preliminary measure against trademark infringement.[621] Meanwhile, Article 12(2) of Internet Address Resource Act provides, 'When anyone registers, possesses or uses a domain name in violation of paragraph (1),[622] the lawful right holder may demand deletion or "transfer" of such domain name.' Unlawful Registration or exercise of such domain name is not subject to criminal sanction in Unfair Competition Act.[623]

---

617. Unfair Competition Act, Art. 2. 1. (g).
618. Unfair Competition Act, Art. 2. 1. (h).
619. Unfair Competition Act, Art. 5.
620. Unfair Competition Act, Art. 4(1) 3.
621. SCt. 2008. 9. 25 – 2006 Da 51577.
622. (1) No one shall obstruct the registration of domain name by lawful right holder. No one shall register, possess or use domain name for unjust purposes, such as reaping illegal profits from lawful right holder.
623. Refer to Unfair Competition Act, Art. 18(3) 1.

6. Copying the Figure of Other's Goods[624]

478. Any act of transferring, renting, exhibiting, importing, or exporting goods whose figure has been copied from the goods manufactured by another person conforms to this provision. The 'figure' here refers to the form, image, colour, gloss, or any combination of these and includes the shape of any test product, the shape in goods brochure. For only domestically well-known identities are subjects of Unfair Competition Act, the figures of goods below such standard is left out of protection, leaving third parties unjust imitation uncontrolled. In addition, many commercial goods have short life span and susceptible to fashion. For such figures, seeking for design protection which entails examination and registration is unsuitable. Unfair Competition Act instituted this rule to protect said figures laid in dead zone of protection between Unfair Competition Act and Design Protection Act.

479. On the other side, either of the following acts shall be excluded from said regulation:

(1) An act of transferring, renting, exhibiting, importing, or exporting goods whose figure was counterfeited, but three years elapsed from the counterfeited goods initial completion.
(2) An act of transferring, renting, exhibiting, importing, or exporting goods whose figure was counterfeited, but the figure is ordinary one for goods of such function or utility.

II. Supplementary Types of Unfair Competition Deeds[625]

480. Any act other than Article 2. 1. (a) through (i), which unfairly appropriates the result of other's endeavour or investment for his/her commercial purpose conforms this provision. This is a 'catch-all provision' to cope with new types of unfair competition act which may emerge along with technological development etc. Though it is newly stipulated as a type of unfair competition through amendment of 2013, courts have regarded such deeds to constitute torts in Civil Law, disposing supplementary position of unfair competition act.

§3. REMEDIES

I. Prohibition Order (Injunction)[626]

481. A person whose business interest is injured or threatened by an act of unfair competition (hereinafter, referred as 'right holder') may seek a court prohibition

624. Unfair Competition Act, Art. 2. 1. (i).
625. Unfair Competition Act, Art. 2. 1. (j).
626. Unfair Competition Act, Art. 4.

order or preventive order against a person who engages in an act of unfair competition. Where right holder demands prohibition order, he/she may demand the destruction of products by which infringement was committed, the removal of the facilities used for the act of infringement, deletion of infringing domain name, or other necessary measures.

II. Damages

482. Any type of unfair competition act (infringement) is an act of 'tort'. Damages are available to torts of wilfulness or negligence in accordance with relevant provisions in Civil Act.[627] However, in most cases, it is hard for plaintiff to prove causal relation between infringement and actual damages. To alleviate this problem and protect plaintiff effectively, Unfair Competition Act provides several special articles of damage calibration rules, which are based upon some legal presumptions.

A. *'Number of Transferred Articles by Infringer' X 'Right Holder's Profit per Unit'*[628]

483. In measuring damages, the amount of losses may be calculated by multiplying 'the number of articles infringer transferred' by 'the right holder's possible profit per unit of the article'. In such cases, the compensation shall be determined between the amount that right holder's total capability of sales would have produced as maximum, and the amount that right holder actually has sold under circumstance of infringement. Where defendant successfully attests the amount that plaintiff would not have obtained even without infringement, such amount shall be deducted from aforesaid damage amount.

B. *Presumption of Infringer's Profit to Damages*[629]

484. If infringer has gained any profit by infringement, the relevant amount of profit shall be presumed as the amount of damages sustained by right holder. As with Article 14-2 (1), this provision is regarded applicable only where right holder produces or sales goods by himself/herself.[630] Whereas the structure of provision seems more straightforward than Article 14-2 (1), it is generally hard for plaintiff to prove 'profit' of defendant.

627. Civil Act, Art. 750.
628. Unfair Competition Act, Art. 14-2(1).
629. Unfair Competition Act, Art. 14-2(2).
630. SCt. 2008. 11. 13 – 2006 Da 22722.

C. *Reasonable Royalty*[631]

485. Plaintiff may choose the amount of reasonable royalty as damages against infringement. For the damages of Article 14-2(1) or (2), the court may exercise its discretion, deducting it if not wilful infringement or of gross negligence.[632] In contrast with it, there is no space of discretion and the reasonable royalty is guaranteed as base amount of damages for every infringement. The reasonable royalty here denotes objective amount of money which would have been paid if infringer had gone into a license contract with right holder. If any case of prior license exists, the actual amount of royalty may be standard; if no such case exists, the practical royalty in the field of work will be criteria.

D. *Decision of Damages by Discretion*[633]

486. Where it is difficult to decide damages by Article 14-2(1) through (3), court may fix considerable damages on its discretion in the light of total purport and evidence in litigation. This is supplemental rule provided for plaintiff who evidently suffered damages by infringement but eventually failed to prove any of its amounts.

III. Return of Unjust Enrichment

487. Right holder may seek for return of unjust enrichment caused by infringement selectively with damages. The option of 'return of unjust enrichment' is merited for plaintiff in light of extinctive prescription (long term of ten years, while that of damages is short term of three years). On the other hand, there is no applicability of presumption rules of Article 14-2; plaintiff bears heavy burden of proof for causation between infringement and defendant's enrichment.

IV. Recovery of Reputation[634]

488. Upon request of right holder, court may order the infringer who has injured the business reputation of right holder to take necessary measures to restore the business reputation.

V. Criminal Sanctions

489. In Korea, the unfair competition acts of, confusing source identity of goods, causing confusion with other's business, damaging the distinctiveness or reputation

631. Unfair Competition Act, Art. 14-2(3).
632. Unfair Competition Act, Art. 14-2(4).
633. Unfair Competition Act, Art. 14-2(5).
634. Unfair Competition Act, Art. 6.

of prominent identification, false indication of origin place, arousing public confusion about place of production or process, arousing misconception for quality of goods etc., and unjustifiable use of mark by agent,[635] are subject to criminal sanctions of imprisonment for not more than three years or by a fine not exceeding KRW 30 million.[636]

635. Unfair Competition Act, Art. 2(1) (a) through (g).
636. Unfair Competition Act, Art. 18(3) 1.

Selected Bibliography

§1. Intellectual Property in General

I. Books

Patent Court. *Intellectual Property Law Litigation Practice*, 3rd edn. Seoul, Korea: Pakyoungsa, 2014.

Yoon, Sunhee. *Intellectual Property Law*, 14th edn. Seoul, Korea: Sechang Publishing Co. 2014.

II. Article

Park, Joonseok. 'The Past, Present, and Future of the Korean Intellectual Property Law', *Justice* 136, (2013): 121.

§2. Copyright

I. Books

Lee, Haewan. *Copyright Law.* Seoul, Korea: Pakyoungsa, 2012.

Oh, Seungjong. *Copyright Law.* Seoul, Korea: Pakyoungsa, 2013.

Park, Seongho. *Copyright Law.* Seoul, Korea: Pakyoungsa, 2014.

II. Articles

Cho, Youngsun. 'Statutory Damages for Copyright Infringement -A Study on Art. 125-2 of Recently Amended Korean Copyright Law'. *Bupjo* 61 no. 4 (2012): 122.

Cho, Youngsun. 'A Proposal of Copyright Act Revision for Employee's Work Provision'. *Copyright Quarterly* 26, no. 3 (2013): 34.

Cho, Youngsun. 'A Study on Innocent Copyright Infringement'. *Justice* 142 (2014): 125.

Lee, Haewan. 'The Problems of Trust Based Collective Copyright Management System and Legislative Alternative'*Bupjo* 59, no. 4 (2010): 151.

Oh, Seungjong. 'A Study on the Substantial Similarity Requirement in Copyright Infringement'. *Comparative Private Laws* 10, no. 2 (2003): 449.
Oh, Seungjong. 'Some Studies on Joint Copyright and Joint Neighboring Right'. *Creations & Rights* 65 (2011): 89.
Park, Seongho. 'Transformation of Personality Rights: Focusing on the Issue of 'Right of Publicity'. *Buphak-Nonchong* 23, no. 2 (2006): 385.
Park, Joonseok. 'Is it Illegal to Download Illegal Material from Internet?-In Relation to the Requirement of Reproduction for Private Use Exception in Korean Copyright Act'. *Bupjo* 59, no. 1 (2010): 241.

§3. Patents

I. Books

Cho, Youngsun. *Patent Law, 4th edn.* Seoul, Korea: Pakyoungsa, 2013.
Jung, Sangjo & Park, Sungsoo. *Commentary on Korean Patent Law*. Seoul, Korea: Pakyoungsa, 2010.
Patent Court. *Intellectual Property Law Litigation Practice*, 3rd edn. Seoul, Korea: Pakyoungsa, 2014.

II. Articles

Cho, Youngsun. 'The Reasonable Remuneration for Employee Invention and Patent Invalidity', *Justice* 129 (2012): 164.
Cho, Youngsun. 'Legal Issues on Patent Infringement by Multiple Parties'. *Bupjo* 57, no. 10 (2008): 208.
Cho, Youngsun. 'Civil Law Issues Pertaining to Patent Invalidation. *Bupjo* 55, no. 3 (2006): 61.
Cho, Youngsun. 'Person Having Ordinary Skill in the Art in Patent Litigation – Proposal of Two New Aspects'. *Justice* 86 (2005): 64.
Cho, Youngsun. 'Redesign of Patent Right Abuse Dogma'. *Justice* 135 (2013): 137.
Cho, Youngsun, 'Analysis and Proposal for 'Inventor's Right to Be Patented' Provisions in Korean Patent Act'. *Korea L.R.* 63 (2011): 73.
Cho, Youngsun. 'Legal Issues of Patent Co-ownership -Interpretation of §99 and Proposal of Amendment-'. *Bupjo* 60, no. 3 (2011): 43.
Cho, Youngsun. 'The Experimental Use of Patented Invention and the Limitations of Patent Right'. *Justice* 116 (2010): 41.
Cho, Youngsun. 'The Requisite of Patent Claim Support by Description'. *Korea L.R.* 66 (2012): 273.
Kwon, Taebok. 'Arguments Based on Prior Use and Public Use in Patent Infringement Actions'. *Industrial Property Right* 34 (2011): 57.
Shin, Heyeun. 'The Description Requirements for a Selective Invention -Focused on the Supreme Court's Decision 2008Hu736, Delivered on December 15th 2009'. *Creations & Rights* 68 (2012): 2.

§4. Trademark / Unfair Competition

I. Books

Moon, Samsup. *Trademark Act*. Seoul, Korea: Sechang Publishing Co, 2004.

Patent Court. *Intellectual Property Law Litigation Practice*, 3rd edn. Seoul, Korea: Pakyoungsa, 2014.

Yoon, Sunhee & Kim Jiyoung. *Unfair Competition Act*. Seoul, Korea: Bupmunsa, 2012.

II. Articles

Cho, Youngsun. 'Review of Trademark Use Notion in Korean Trademark Law in Enactive Approach'. *Justice* 105 (2008): 128.

Cho, Youngsun. 'Defense of Trademark Invalidity in Trademark Infringement Litigations'. *Justice* 125 (2011): 54.

Cho, Youngsun. 'Rethinking the Remedies for Trademark Infringement -Focusing on Simple negligence Immunity'. *Bupjo* 62, no. 8 (2013): 45.

Jeong Sangjo. 'Conflicts between Well-Known Marks and Registered Marks'. *Seoul L.J.* 43, no. 4 (2002): 129.

Lee, SangJung. 'A Study on the Amended Provisions of The Unfair Competition Prevention and Trade Secret Protection Act'. *Creations & Rights* 73 (2013): 96.

§5. Industrial Design

I. Book

Roh, Taejung. *Design Protection Act*. Seoul, Korea: Sechang Publishing Co. 2014.

II. Articles

Kim, WonO. Contending Issues of Korea-EU FTA in the Field of Trademark and Design Protection. *Industrial Property Right* 26 (2008): 31.

Kim, WonO. The Problem of a 'Cumulation of Protection System' and Its Solution. *Industrial Property Right* 15 (2004): 121.

Selected Bibliography

§6. Trade Secret: Confidential Information

I. Book

Lee, Yoonwon. *Trade Secret Protection Act.* Seoul, Korea: Pakyoungsa, 2012.

II. Articles

Kwon, Taebok. 'Idea Protection System in Intellectual Property Right' *Industrial Property Right* 41 (2013):1.

Park, Joonseok. 'The Comparative Analysis on the Trade Secret Protection in Korea'*Industrial Property Right* 38 (2012):1.

Index

The numbers here refer to paragraph numbers.

Abuse of Trademark Right, 322
Acquisition of Distinctiveness, 292
Acts Deemed Infringement, 121, 122, 123, 335, 425
Adjudication for Grant, 217
Advantageous Effects, 165
Aesthetic Impression, 367
Amendment, 190
Applied Arts, 29
Appointment of Judges, 11
Art in Public Domain, 229, 240
Article, 365
Attribution Right, 48, 68

Breeder's right, 418, 420
Broadcasting, 58, 77
Broadcasting Service Provider, 104
Business Emblem, 279
Business Method, 148, 170

Cancellation upon Inappropriate Use, 354
Cancellation upon Non-Use, 355
Certification Mark, 280
Chip Protection, 431
Cinematographic Work, 28
Civil Proceedings, 12
Claim Interpretation, 209, 210, 211
Claims, 172
Collective Mark, 276
Commencement of Examination, 188
Compilation Work, 27
Compulsory License, 90, 215, 216, 217
Computer Program, 30, 85, 123, 144
Continuous Use, 292, 293
Converted Application, 192
Copyright, 19
Creativity, 35

Damages, 127, 245, 339, 360, 396, 426, 448, 462, 482
Database, 31
De Facto Standard, 37
Deceptive Mark, 304
Defaming Use of a Work, 51
Denomination, 413
Derivation, 197, 198
Derivative Work, 26, 66
Descriptive Mark, 287
Descriptive Use, 319
Design, 363
Designated Goods, 282
Detail Description, 176, 179, 210
Digital Audio Transmission, 60
Disclosure Right, 47
Disclosure upon Request, 383
Disparaging Marks, 295
Distinctiveness, 284, 291
Distinctness, 410
Distribution, 62
Divisional Application, 191
Doctrine of Equivalents, 224
Domain Name, 330, 477
Domestic Priority Claim, 194
Double Patent, 214
Duration of Protection, 94, 220, 333, 392, 423, 446
Duty to Report Arts Relevant with Invention, 180

Employee's Invention, 199
Employee's Work, 42
Enlarged Concept of Novelty, 157
Equivalent Infringement, 224
Exhaustion, 63, 235, 327, 422, 443
Exhibition, 61, 87
Expropriation, 215

Fair Use, 89
Figure of Other's Goods, 478
First to File, 184, 311

Functional Claim, 173
Functional Mark, 308, 321
Functional Work, 36

Generic Term, 285
Geographical Collective Mark, 277
Geographical Name, 288
Governmental Works, 23
Group Design, 381

Immunity for Bona Fide Person, 444
Incremental Invention, 231
Indirect Infringement, 81, 115, 234, 336, 394
Industrial Applicability, 149, 372
Industrial Designs, 362
Injunction, 126, 243, 338, 395, 424, 447, 461, 481
Integrity Right, 49, 69
Internet Transmission, 59
Invalidation Trial, 263
Invalidity Defence, 239, 324
Invention, 138
Inventive Step, 158

Joint Authorship, 40

Laying-Open of Application, 187
Layout-Design, 431, 441
License, 45, 205, 206, 315, 387, 419, 439, 440
Lineage of Unfair Acquirement, 455, 456, 457
Lineage of Unfair Disclosure, 458, 459, 460
Literal Infringement, 223
Loss of Distinctiveness, 293

Mark against Public Order, 297
Medical Skills, 150
Micro-Organisms, 145
Moral Rights, 46

Neighboring Rights, 101
New Matter Addition, 186
New Use Invention, 167
New Use of Known Matter, 142
News Reports, 24, 73
Nonboviousness, 158, 375, 376
Non-Prejudicial Disclosures, 155, 374
Novelty, 153, 373, 409
Numeral Limitation Invention, 169, 183

Online Service Provider, 119

Parallel Import, 64, 327
Partial Design, 368
Partial Examination, 384
Patent, 137
Performers, 102
Person Skilled in the Art, 161, 179
Plagiarism, 55
Plant Variety, 407
Popular Name, 289
Prior User's Right, 213, 325, 391
Priority Claim under Treaty, 193
Product by Process Claim, 175
Program Language, 25
Prohibition Order, 126, 243, 338, 481, 395, 424, 447, 461
Property Rights of Copyright, 53
Prosecution History, 211, 230
Provisional Application, 178
Provisional Protection, 416
Public Performance, 56, 78
Public Transmission, 57

Quotation, 75

Reasonable Royalty, 129, 248, 342, 399, 450, 485
Recovery of Reputation, 251, 347, 403, 427, 488
Relevant Design, 379
Rental Right, 65
Reproduction, 54, 87
Reproduction for Private Use, 79
Right to Obtain Patent, 195
Rights Management Information, 125

Scènes à Faire, 38
School Education, 72
Searching Keywords, 330
Secondary Considerations, 166
Secret Design, 380
Selection Invention, 143, 168, 182, 233
Service Mark, 274
Simple And Ordinary Mark, 290
Soribada Case, 82, 116
Sound Recording Producer, 103
Specification, 171
Stability, 412
Statutory Damages, 131, 344
Submission of Copy, 98
Submission Order of Documents, 254

Technical Protection Measures, 124
Temporary Reproduction, 88
Trade Secret, 454
Trademark, 274
Trademark Use, 328
Transfer of Rights, 44, 204, 314, 386, 418, 438
Trial against Rejection to Application, 262
Trial for Correction, 265
Trial for Granting Non-exclusive License, 218
Trial to Confirm the Scope of Right, 264
Tribunal in KIPO, 15
Typeface, 369

Unfair Competition, 241, 273, 323, 466
Uniformity, 411
Use Prior to Registration, 451
User's Name, 318
Utility Models, 269

Working of Patented Invention, 207
Works, 21
Works against Order of Public, 33

Index

www.ingramcontent.com/pod-product-compliance
Lightning Source LLC
Chambersburg PA
CBHW071448230926
51846CB00001B/379
* 9 7 8 9 0 4 1 1 6 0 0 9 6 *